IT DOESN'T HAVE TO BE CRAZY AT WORK

80-hour weeks
Packed schedules
Super busy
Endless meetings
Overflowing inbox
Unrealistic deadlines
Can't sleep
Sunday-afternoon emails
No time to think
Stuck at the office
All-nighters
Chats blowing up

IT DOESN'T HAVE TO BE CRAZY AT WORK
BY JASON FRIED AND DAVID HEINEMEIER HANSSON OF BASECAMP

HARPER
BUSINESS

An Imprint of HarperCollinsPublishers

Contents

Feed Your Culture

Dissect Your Process

Mind Your Business

Last

First

It's crazy at work

How often have you heard someone say "It's crazy at work"? Maybe you've even said it yourself. For many, "It's crazy at work" has become their normal. But why so crazy?

There are two primary reasons: (1) The workday is being sliced into tiny, fleeting work moments by an onslaught of physical and virtual distractions. And (2) an unhealthy obsession with growth at any cost sets towering, unrealistic expectations that stress people out.

It's no wonder people are working longer, earlier, later, on weekends, and whenever they have a spare moment. People can't get work done at work anymore. That turns life into work's leftovers. The doggie bag.

What's worse is that long hours, excessive busyness, and lack of sleep have become a badge of honor for many people these days. Sustained exhaustion is not a badge of honor, it's a mark of stupidity.

And it's not just about organizations—individuals, contractors, and solopreneurs are burning themselves out in the very same way.

You'd think that with all the hours people are putting in, and all the promises of new technologies, the load would be lessening. It's not. It's getting heavier.

But the thing is, there's not more work to be done all of a sudden. The problem is that there's hardly any uninterrupted, dedicated time to do it. People are working more but getting less done. It doesn't add up—until you account for the majority of time being wasted on things that don't matter.

Out of the 60, 70, or 80 hours a week many people are expected to pour into work, how many of those hours are really spent on the work itself? And how many are tossed away in meetings, lost to distraction, and withered away by inefficient business practices? The bulk of them.

The answer isn't more hours, it's less bullshit. Less waste, not more production. And far fewer distractions, less always-on anxiety, and avoiding stress.

Stress is passed from organization to employee, from employee to employee, and then from employee to customer. Stress never stops at the border of work, either. It bleeds into life. It infects your relationships with your friends, your family, your kids.

The promises keep coming. More time-management hacks. More ways to communicate. And new demands keep piling up. To pay attention to more conversations in more places, to respond within minutes. Faster and faster, for what?

If it's constantly crazy at work, we have two words for you: Fuck that. And two more: Enough already.

It's time for companies to stop asking their employees to breathlessly chase ever-higher, ever-more-artificial targets set by ego. It's time to give people the uninterrupted time that great work demands. It's time to stop celebrating crazy at work.

For nearly 20 years we've been working at making Basecamp a calm company. One that isn't fueled by stress, or ASAP, or rushing, or late nights, or all-nighter crunches, or impossible promises, or high turnover, or consistently missed deadlines, or projects that never seem to end.

No growth-at-all-costs. No false busyness. No ego-driven goals. No keeping up with the Joneses Corporation. No hair on fire. And yet we've been profitable every year we've been in business.

We're in one of the most competitive industries in the world. In addition to tech giants, the software industry is dominated by startups backed by hundreds of millions of dollars in venture capital. We've taken zero. Where does our money come from? Customers. Call us old-fashioned.

As a software company, we're supposed to be playing the hustle game in Silicon Valley, but we don't have a single employee in the Valley. In fact, our staff of 54 is spread out across about 30 different cities around the world.

We put in about 40 hours a week most of the year and just 32 in the summer. We send people on month-long sabbaticals every three years. We not only pay for people's vacation time, we pay for the actual vacation, too.

No, not 9 p.m. Wednesday night. It can wait until 9 a.m. Thursday morning. No, not Sunday. Monday.

Are there occasionally stressful moments? Sure—such is life. Is every day peachy? Of course not—we'd be lying if we said it was. But we do our best to make sure those are the exceptions. On balance we're calm—by choice, by practice. We're intentional about it. We've made different decisions from the rest.

We've designed our company differently. We're here to tell you about the choices we've made and why we've made many of them. There's a path for any company willing to make similar choices. You've got to want it, but if you do you'll realize it's much nicer over here. You can have a calm company, too.

The modern workplace is sick. Chaos should not be the natural state at work. Anxiety isn't a prerequisite for progress. Sitting in meetings all day isn't required for success. These are all perversions of work—side effects of broken models and follow-the-lemming-off-the-cliff worst practices. Step aside and let the suckers jump.

Calm is protecting people's time and attention.

Calm is about 40 hours of work a week.

Calm is reasonable expectations.

Calm is ample time off.

Calm is smaller.

Calm is a visible horizon.

Calm is meetings as a last resort.

Calm is asynchronous first, real-time second.

Calm is more independence, less interdependence.

Calm is sustainable practices for the long term.

Calm is profitability.

A quick bit about us

We're Jason and David. We've been running Basecamp together since 2003. Jason is CEO, David is CTO, and we're the only two Cs at the company.

Basecamp is both the name of our company and the name of our product. The Basecamp product is a unique cloud-based application that helps companies organize all their projects and internal communications in one place. When everything's in Basecamp, people know what they need to do, everyone knows where everything is, it's easy to see where things stand, and nothing slips through the cracks.

We've experimented a lot with how we run our business. In this book we share what's worked for us, along with observations and realizations about what makes for a healthy, long-term, sustainable business. As with all advice, your mileage may vary. Take these ideas as inspiration for change, not as some sort of divine doctrine.

Lastly, we use the word "crazy" in this book in the same way people use crazy to describe the crazy traffic at rush hour, the crazy weather outside, and the crazy line at the airport. When we say crazy, we're calling situations crazy, not people.

With that, let's get started.

Your company is a product

It begins with this idea: Your company is a product.

Yes, the things you make are products (or services), but your company is the thing that makes those things. That's why your company should be your best product.

Everything in this book revolves around that idea. That, like product development, progress is achieved through iteration. If you want to make a product better, you have to keep tweaking, revising, and iterating. The same thing is true with a company.

But when it comes to companies, many stand still. They might change what they make, but how they make it stays the same. They choose a way to work once and stick with it. Whatever workplace fad is hot when they get started becomes ingrained and permanent. Policies are set in cement. Companies get stuck with themselves.

But when you think of the company as a product, you ask different questions: Do people who work here know how to use the company? Is it simple? Complex? Is it obvious how it works? What's fast about it? What's slow about it? Are there bugs?

What's broken that we can fix quickly and what's going to take a long time?

A company is like software. It has to be usable, it has to be useful. And it probably also has bugs, places where the company crashes because of bad organizational design or cultural oversights.

When you start to think about your company as a product, all sorts of new possibilities for improvement emerge. When you realize the way you work is malleable, you can start molding something new, something better.

We work on projects for six weeks at a time, then we take two weeks off from scheduled work to roam and decompress. We didn't simply theorize that would be the best way to work. We started by working on things for as long as they took. Then we saw how projects never seemed to end. So we started time-boxing at three months. We found that was still too long. So we tried even shorter times. And we ended up here, in six-week cycles. We iterated our way to what works for us. We'll talk all about this in the book.

We didn't just assume asynchronous communication is better than real-time communication most of the time. We figured it out after overusing chat tools for years. We discovered how the distractions went up and the work went down. So we figured out a better way to communicate. We'll talk all about this in the book.

We didn't launch with the benefits we have today. We worked our way toward them. We didn't realize paying for people's vacations was better than cash bonuses. We started with the latter and realized that bonuses were just taken as an expected part of pay, anyway. We applied that experience to other benefits. We'll talk all about this in the book.

We didn't start with a calm approach to salary negotiations; we worked our way here. Setting salaries and granting raises was as stressful at Basecamp as it is at most other companies. Until we iterated our way to a new method. We'll talk all about this in the book.

We work on our company as hard as we work on our products. People often toss a version number at the end of software. "This is iOS 10.1, 10.2, 10.5, 11, etc. . . ." We think of our company in the same way. Today's Basecamp, LLC, is like version 50.3 of Basecamp, LLC. We got here by going there, trying that, and figuring out what works best.

Running a calm company is, unfortunately, not the default way to run a company these days. You have to work against your instincts for a while. You have to put toxic industry norms aside. You have to recognize that "It's crazy at work" isn't right. Calm is a destination and we'll share with you how we got there and stay there.

Our company is a product. We want you to think of yours as one, too. Whether you own it, run it, or "just" work there, it takes everyone involved to make it better.

BRITISH NATURALIST CHARLES DARWIN PUBLISHED 19 BOOKS, INCLUDING "ON THE ORIGIN OF SPECIES," WHILE WORKING JUST 4.5 HOURS A DAY.

Curb Your Ambition

Bury the hustle

Hustlemania has captured a monopoly on entrepreneurial inspiration. This endless stream of pump-me-up quotes about working yourself to the bone. It's time to snap out of it.

Just have a look at the #entrepreneur tag on Instagram. "Legends are born in a valley of struggle!"; "You don't have to be ridiculously gifted, you just have to be ridiculously committed"; and "Your goals don't care how you feel." Yeah, it just keeps going like this until you're ready to puke.

The hustle may have started as a beacon for those with little to outsmart those with a lot, but now it's just synonymous with *the grind*.

And for everyone in that tiny minority that somehow finds what they're looking for in the grind, there are so many more who end up broken, wasted, and burned out with nothing to show for it. And for what?

You aren't more worthy in defeat or victory because you sacrificed everything. Because you kept pushing through the pain and exhaustion for a bigger carrot. The human experience is so much more than 24/7 hustle to the max.

It's also just bad advice. You're not very likely to find that key insight or breakthrough idea north of the 14th hour in the day. Creativity, progress, and impact do not yield to brute force.

Now this opposition mainly comes from a lens focused on the world of creative people. The writers, the programmers, the designers, the makers, the product people. There are probably manual-labor domains where greater input does equal greater output, at least for a time.

But you rarely hear about people working three low-end jobs out of necessity wearing that grind with pride. It's only the pretenders, those who aren't exactly struggling for subsistence, who feel the need to brag about their immense sacrifice.

Entrepreneurship doesn't have to be this epic tale of cutthroat survival. Most of the time it's way more boring than that. Less jumping over exploding cars and wild chase scenes, more laying of bricks and applying another layer of paint.

So you hereby have our permission to bury the hustle. To put in a good day's work, day after day, but nothing more. You can play with your kids and still be a successful entrepreneur. You can have a hobby. You can take care of yourself physically. You can read a book. You can watch a silly movie with your partner. You can take the time to cook a proper meal. You can go for a long walk. You can dare to be completely ordinary every now and then.

Happy pacifists

The business world is obsessed with fighting and winning and dominating and destroying. This ethos turns business leaders into tiny Napoleons. It's not enough for them to merely put their dent in the universe. No, they have to fucking own the universe.

Companies that live in such a zero-sum world don't "earn market share" from a competitor, they "conquer the market." They don't just serve their customers, they "capture" them. They "target" customers, employ a sales "force," hire "headhunters" to find new talent, pick their "battles," and make a "killing."

This language of war writes awful stories. When you think of yourself as a military commander who has to eliminate the enemy (your competition), it's much easier to justify dirty tricks and anything-goes morals. And the bigger the battle, the dirtier it gets.

Like they say, all's fair in love and war. Except this isn't love, and it isn't war. It's business.

Sadly, it's not easy to escape the business tropes of war and conquest. Every media outlet has a template for describing rival companies as warring factions. Sex sells, wars sell, and business battles serve as financial-page porn.

But that paradigm just doesn't make any sense to us.

We come in peace. We don't have imperial ambitions. We aren't trying to dominate an industry or a market. We wish everyone well. To get ours, we don't need to take theirs.

What's our market share? Don't know, don't care. It's irrelevant. Do we have enough customers paying us enough money to cover our costs and generate a profit? Yes. Is that number increasing every year? Yes. That's good enough for us. Doesn't matter if we're 2 percent of the market or 4 percent or 75 percent. What matters is that we have a healthy business with sound economics that work for us. Costs under control, profitable sales.

Further, as far as market share goes, you'd need to define the market size accurately to define your share of it. As of the printing of this book, we have more than 100,000 companies that pay on a monthly basis for Basecamp. And that generates tens of millions of dollars in annual profit for us. We're pretty sure that's barely a blip of the overall market and that's just fine with us. We're serving our customers well, and they're serving us well. That's what matters. Doubling, tripling, quadrupling our market share doesn't matter.

Lots of companies are driven by comparisons in general. Not just whether they're first, second, or third in their industry, but how they stack up feature for feature with their closest competitors. Who's getting which awards? Who's raising more money? Who's getting all the press? Why are they sponsoring that conference and not us?

Mark Twain nailed it: "Comparison is the death of joy." We're with Mark.

We don't compare. What others do has no bearing on what we're able to do, what we want to do, or what we choose to do. There's no chase at Basecamp, no rabbit to pursue. Just a deep satisfaction with doing our very best work as measured by our happiness and our customers' purchases.

The only things we're out to destroy are outmoded ideas.

The opposite of conquering the world isn't failure, it's participation. Being one of many options in a market is a virtue that allows customers to have a real choice. If you can embrace that, then the war metaphors of business can more easily be buried, as they should be.

Because at the end of the day, would you rather win an imaginary contest by throwing sand in your competitors' faces or by simply forgetting about them and making the best damn product you know how?

Our goal: No goals

Quarterly goals. Yearly goals. Big Hairy Audacious Goals.

"We grew 14 percent last quarter, so let's aim for 25 percent growth this time."

"Let's hire our one hundredth employee this year."

"Let's get that cover story so they'll finally take us seriously."

The wisdom of setting business goals—always striving for bigger and better—is so established that it seems like the only thing left to debate is whether the goals are ambitious enough.

So imagine the response when we tell people that we don't do goals. At all. No customer-count goals, no sales goals, no retention goals, no revenue goals, no specific profitability goals (other than to be profitable). Seriously.

This anti-goal mindset definitely makes Basecamp an outcast in the business world. Part of the minority, the ones who simply "don't get how it works."

We get how it works—we just don't care. We don't mind leaving some money on the table and we don't need to squeeze every drop out of the lemon. Those final drops usually taste sour, anyway.

Are we interested in increasing profits? Yes. Revenues? Yes. Being more effective? Yes. Making our products easier, faster, and more useful? Yes. Making our customers and employees happier? Yes, absolutely. Do we love iterating and improving? Yup!

Do we want to make things better? All the time. But do we want to maximize "better" through constantly chasing goals? No thanks.

That's why we don't have goals at Basecamp. We didn't when we started, and now, nearly 20 years later, we still don't. We simply do the best work we can on a daily basis.

But there was a brief moment when we changed our mind. We pinned up a big round revenue target—one of those fat nine-digit numbers. "Why not?" we thought. "We can do it!" But after chasing that goal for a while, we thought again. And the answer to "Why not?" became a very clear "Because (1) it's disingenuous for us to pretend we care about a number we just made up, and (2) because we aren't willing to make the cultural compromises it'll take to get there."

Because let's face it: Goals are fake. Nearly all of them are artificial targets set for the sake of setting targets. These made-up numbers then function as a source of unnecessary stress until they're either achieved or abandoned. And when that happens, you're supposed to pick new ones and start stressing again. Nothing ever stops at the quarterly win. There are four quarters to a year. Forty to a decade. Every one of them has to produce, exceed, and beat EXPECTATIONS.

Why would you do that to yourself and your business? Doing great, creative work is hard enough. So is building a long-lasting sustainable business with happy employees. So why impose some arbitrary number to loom over your job, salary, bonus, and kid's college fund?

Plus, there's an even darker side to goal setting. Chasing goals often leads companies to compromise their morals, honesty, and integrity to reach those fake numbers. The best intentions slip when you're behind. Need to improve margins by a few points? Let's turn a blind eye to quality for a while. Need to find another $800,000 this quarter to hit that number? Let's make it harder for customers to request refunds.

Ever try to cancel an account with your cell phone company? It's not an inherently complicated act. But many phone companies make it so difficult to do because they have retention goals to hit. They want to make it hard for you to cancel so it's easier for them to hit their numbers.

Even we weren't immune to those pressures. In the few months that we tried reaching for the big nine-digit goal, we ended up launching several projects that at best we had misgivings about and at worst made us feel a little dirty. Like spending big bucks with Facebook, Twitter, and Google to juice our signups. Cutting checks like that to further the erosion of privacy and splintering of attention just made us feel icky, but we closed our eyes for a while because, hey, we were reaching for that big number. Fuck that.

How about something really audacious: No targets, no goals?

You can absolutely run a great business without a single goal. You don't need something fake to do something real. And if you must have a goal, how about just staying in business? Or serving your customers well? Or being a delightful place to work? Just because these goals are harder to quantify does not make them any less important.

ATUL GAWANDE, A SURGEON WHO'S WRITTEN FOUR BESTSELLING BOOKS, BLOCKS OFF 25% OF HIS TIME FOR UNSCHEDULED BUT IMPORTANT TASKS TO AVOID GETTING SWALLOWED UP BY EMAIL AND MEETINGS.

Don't change the world

The business world is suffering from ambition hyperinflation. It's no longer about simply making a great product or providing a great service. No, now it's all about how this BRAND-NEW THING CHANGES EVERYTHING. A thousand revolutions promised all at once. Come on.

Nothing encapsulates this like the infatuation with disruption. Everyone wants to be a disrupter these days. Break all the rules (and several laws). Upend every existing industry. But if you label your own work as disruption, it probably isn't.

Basecamp isn't changing the world. It's making it easier for companies and teams to communicate and collaborate. That's absolutely worthwhile and it makes for a wonderful business, but we're not exactly rewriting world history. And that's okay.

If you stop thinking that you must change the world, you lift a tremendous burden off yourself and the people around you. There's no longer this convenient excuse for why it has to be all work all the time. The opportunity to do another good day's work will come again tomorrow, even if you go home at a reasonable time.

So it becomes much harder to justify those 9 p.m. meetings or weekend sprints. And, as an added bonus, you won't sound like a delusional braggart when you describe what you do at the next family get-together. "What do I do? Oh, I work at PetEmoji— we're changing the world by disrupting the pet health-care insurance space." Riiiiight.

Set out to do good work. Set out to be fair in your dealings with customers, employees, and reality. Leave a lasting impression with the people you touch and worry less (or not at all!) about changing the world. Chances are, you won't, and if you do, it's not going to be because you said you would.

Make it up as you go

We don't do grand plans at Basecamp—not for the company, not for the product. There's no five-year plan. No three-year plan. No one-year plan. Nada.

We didn't start the business with a plan, and we don't run the business by a plan. For nearly 20 years, we've been figuring it out as we go, a few weeks at a time.

For some that may seem shortsighted. They'd be right. We're literally looking at what's in front of us, not at everything we could possibly imagine.

Short-term planning has gotten a bum rap, but we think it's undeserved. Every six weeks or so, we decide what we'll be working on next. And that's the only plan we have. Anything further out is considered a "maybe, we'll see."

When you stick with planning for the short term, you get to change your mind often. And that's a huge relief! This eliminates the pressure for perfect planning and all the stress that comes with it. We simply believe that you're better off steering the ship with a thousand little inputs as you go rather than a few grand sweeping movements made way ahead of time.

Furthermore, long-term planning instills a false sense of security. The sooner you admit you have no idea what the world will look like in five years, three years, or even one year, the sooner you'll be able to move forward without the fear of making the wrong big decision years in advance. Nothing looms when you don't make predictions.

Much corporate anxiety comes from the realization that the company has been doing the wrong thing, but it's too late to change direction because of the "Plan." "We've got to see it through!" Seeing a bad idea through just because at one point it sounded like a good idea is a tragic waste of energy and talent.

The further away you are from something, the fuzzier it becomes. The future is a major abstraction, riddled with a million vibrating variables you can't control. The best information you'll ever have about a decision is at the moment of execution. We wait for those moments to make a call.

Comfy's cool

The idea that you have to *constantly* push yourself out of your comfort zone is the kind of supposedly self-evident nonsense you'll often find in corporate manifestos. That unless you're uncomfortable with what you're doing, you're not trying hard enough, not pushing hard enough. What?

Requiring discomfort—or pain—to make progress is faulty logic. **NO PAIN, NO GAIN!** looks good on a poster at the gym, but work and working out aren't the same. And, frankly, you don't need to hurt yourself to get healthier, either.

Sure, *sometimes* we stand at the threshold of a breakthrough, and taking the last few steps can be *temporarily* uncomfortable or, yes, even painful. But this is the exception, not the rule.

Generally speaking, the notion of having to break out of something to reach the next level doesn't jibe with us. Oftentimes it's not breaking out, but diving in, digging deeper, staying in your rabbit hole that brings the biggest gains. Depth, not breadth, is where mastery is often found.

Most of the time, if you're uncomfortable with something, it's because it isn't right. Discomfort is the human response to a questionable or bad situation, whether that's working long hours with no end in sight, exaggerating your business numbers to impress investors, or selling intimate user data to advertisers. If you get into the habit of suppressing all discomfort, you're going to lose yourself, your manners, and your morals.

On the contrary, if you listen to your discomfort and back off from what's causing it, you're more likely to find the right path. We've been in that place many times over the years at Basecamp.

It was the discomfort of knowing two people doing the same work at the same level were being paid differently that led us to reform how we set salaries. That's how we ended up throwing out individual negotiations and differences in pay, and going with a simpler system.

It was how uncomfortable it felt working for other people at companies that had taken large amounts of venture capital that kept us on the path of profitable independence at Basecamp.

Being comfortable in your zone is essential to being calm.

NOVELIST ISABEL ALLENDE
HAS TWO OFFICES, ONE JUST
FOR WRITING THAT HAS NO
INTERNET OR TELEPHONE, AND
ANOTHER FOR TACKLING
ADMINISTRATIVE TASKS.

Defend Your Time

8's enough, 40's plenty

Working 40 hours a week is plenty. Plenty of time to do great work, plenty of time to be competitive, plenty of time to get the important stuff done.

So that's how long we work at Basecamp. No more. Less is often fine, too. During the summer, we even take Fridays off and still get plenty of good stuff done in just 32 hours.

No all-nighters, no weekends, no "We're in a crunch so we've got to pull 70 or 80 hours this week." Nope.

Those 40-hour weeks are made of 8-hour days. And 8 hours is actually a long time. It takes about 8 hours to fly direct from Chicago to London. Ever been on a transatlantic flight like that? It's a long flight! You think it's almost over, but you check the time and there's still 3 hours left.

Every day your workday is like flying from Chicago to London. But why does the flight feel longer than your time in the office? It's because the flight is uninterrupted, continuous time. It feels long because it *is* long!

Your time in the office feels shorter because it's sliced up into a dozen smaller bits. Most people don't actually have 8 hours a day to work, they have a couple of hours. The rest of the day is stolen from them by meetings, conference calls, and other distractions. So while you may be at the office for 8 hours, it feels more like just a few.

Now you may think cramming all that stuff into 8-hour days and a 40-hour week would be stressful. It's not. Because we don't cram. We don't rush. We don't stuff. We work at a relaxed, sustainable pace. And what doesn't get done in 40 hours by Friday at 5 picks up again Monday morning at 9.

If you can't fit everything you want to do within 40 hours per week, you need to get better at picking what to do, not work longer hours. Most of what we think we *have* to do, we don't have to do at all. It's a choice, and often it's a poor one.

When you cut out what's unnecessary, you're left with what you need. And all you need is 8 hours a day for about 5 days a week.

Protectionism

Companies love to protect.

They protect their brand with trademarks and lawsuits. They protect their data and trade secrets with rules, policies, and NDAs. They protect their money with budgets, CFOs, and investments.

They guard so many things, but all too often they fail to protect what's both most vulnerable and most precious: their employees' time and attention.

Companies spend their employees' time and attention as if there were an infinite supply of both. As if they cost nothing. Yet employees' time and attention are among the scarcest resources we have.

At Basecamp, we see it as our top responsibility to protect our employees' time and attention. You can't expect people to do great work if they don't have a full day's attention to devote to it. Partial attention is barely attention at all.

For example, we don't have status meetings at Basecamp. We all know these meetings—one person talks for a bit and shares some plans, then the next person does the same thing. They're a waste of time. Why? While it seems efficient to get everyone together at the same time, it isn't. It's costly, too. Eight people in a room for an hour doesn't cost one hour, it costs eight hours.

Instead, we ask people to write updates daily or weekly on Basecamp for others to read when they have a free moment. This saves dozens of hours a week and affords people larger blocks of uninterrupted time. Meetings tend to break time into "before" and "after." Get rid of those meetings and people suddenly have a good stretch of time to immerse themselves in their work.

Time and attention are best spent in large bills, if you will, not spare coins and small change. Enough to buy those big chunks of time to do that wonderful, thorough job you're expected to do. When you don't get that, you have to scrounge for focused time, forced to squeeze project work in between all the other nonessential, yet mandated, things you're expected to do every day.

It's no wonder people are coming up short and are working longer hours, late nights, and weekends to make it up. Where else can they find the uninterrupted time? It's sad to think that some people crave a commute because it's the only time during the day they have to themselves.

So, fine, be a protectionist, but remember to protect what matters most.

The quality of an hour

There are lots of ways to slice 60 minutes.

$1 \times 60 = 60$
$2 \times 30 = 60$
$4 \times 15 = 60$
$25 + 10 + 5 + 15 + 5 = 60$

All of the above equal 60, but they're different kinds of hours entirely. The number might be the same, but the quality isn't. The quality hour we're after is 1×60.

A fractured hour isn't really an hour—it's a mess of minutes. It's really hard to get anything meaningful done with such crummy input. A quality hour is 1×60, not 4×15. A quality day is at least 4×60, not $4 \times 15 \times 4$.

It's hard to be effective with fractured hours, but it's easy to be stressed out: 25 minutes on a phone call, then 10 minutes with a colleague who taps you on the shoulder, then 5 on this thing you're supposed to be working on, before another 15 are burned on a conversation you got pulled into that really didn't require your attention. Then you're left with 5 more to do what you wanted to do. No wonder people who work like that can be short- or ill-tempered.

And between all those context switches and attempts at multitasking, you have to add buffer time. Time for your head to leave the last thing and get into the next thing. This is how you end up thinking "What did I actually do today?" when the clock turns to five and you supposedly spent eight hours at the office. You know you were there, but the hours had no weight, so they slipped away with nothing to show.

Look at your hours. If they're a bunch of fractions, who or what is doing the division? Are others distracting you or are you distracting yourself? What can you change? How many things are you working on in a given hour? One thing at a time doesn't mean one thing, then another thing, then another thing in quick succession; it means one big thing for hours at a time or, better yet, a whole day.

Ask yourself: When was the last time you had three or even four completely uninterrupted hours to yourself and your work? When we recently asked a crowd of 600 people at a conference that question, barely 30 hands went up. Would yours have?

PULITZER PRIZE-WINNING AUTHOR COLSON WHITEHEAD WRITES FOR JUST FIVE HOURS A DAY AND TAKES A YEAR OFF BETWEEN PROJECTS TO PLAY VIDEO GAMES AND COOK.

Effective > Productive

Everyone's talking about hacking productivity these days. There's an endless stream of methodologies and tools promising to make you more productive. But more productive at what?

Productivity is for machines, not for people. There's nothing meaningful about packing some number of work units into some amount of time or squeezing more into less.

Machines can work 24/7, humans can't.

When people focus on productivity, they end up focusing on being busy. Filling every moment with something to do. And there's always more to do!

We don't believe in busyness at Basecamp. We believe in effectiveness. How little can we do? How much can we cut out? Instead of adding to-dos, we add to-don'ts.

Being productive is about occupying your time—filling your schedule to the brim and getting as much done as you can. Being effective is about finding more of your time unoccupied and open for other things besides work. Time for leisure, time for family and friends. Or time for doing absolutely nothing.

Yes, it's perfectly okay to have nothing to do. Or, better yet, nothing worth doing. If you've only got three hours of work to do on a given day, then stop. Don't fill your day with five more just to stay busy or feel productive. Not doing something that isn't worth doing is a wonderful way to spend your time.

The outwork myth

You can't outwork the whole world. There's always going to be someone somewhere willing to work as hard as you. Someone just as hungry. Or hungrier.

Assuming you can work harder and longer than someone else is giving yourself too much credit for your effort and not enough for theirs. Putting in 1,001 hours to someone else's 1,000 isn't going to tip the scale in your favor.

What's worse is when management holds up certain people as having a great "work ethic" because they're always around, always available, always working. That's a terrible example of a work ethic and a great example of someone who's overworked.

A great work ethic isn't about working whenever you're called upon. It's about doing what you say you're going to do, putting in a fair day's work, respecting the work, respecting the customer, respecting coworkers, not wasting time, not creating unnecessary work for other people, and not being a bottleneck. Work ethic is about being a fundamentally good person that others can count on and enjoy working with.

So how do people get ahead if it's not about outworking everyone else?

People make it because they're talented, they're lucky, they're
in the right place at the right time, they know how to work with
other people, they know how to sell an idea, they know what
moves people, they can tell a story, they know which details
matter and which don't, they can see the big and small pictures
in every situation, and they know how to do something with an
opportunity. And for so many other reasons.

So get the outwork myth out of your head. Stop equating work
ethic with excessive work hours. Neither is going to get you
ahead or help you find calm.

Work doesn't happen
at work

Ask people where they go when they really need to get something done. One answer you'll rarely hear: the office.

That's right. When you really need to get work done you rarely go into the office. Or, if you must, it's early in the morning, late at night, or on the weekends. All the times when no one else is around. At that point it's not even "the office"—it's just a quiet space where you won't be bothered.

Way too many people simply can't get work done at work anymore.

It doesn't make any sense. Companies pour gobs of money into buying or renting an office and filling it with desks, chairs, and computers. Then they arrange it all so that nobody can actually get anything done there.

Modern-day offices have become interruption factories. Merely walking in the door makes you a target for anyone else's conversation, question, or irritation. When you're on the inside, you're a resource who can be polled, interrogated, or pulled into a meeting. And another meeting about that other meeting. How can you expect anyone to get work done in an environment like that?

It's become fashionable to blame distractions at work on things like Facebook, Twitter, and YouTube. But these things aren't the problem, any more than old-fashioned smoke breaks were the problem 30 years ago. Were cigarettes the problem with work back then?

The major distractions at work aren't from the outside, they're from the inside. The wandering manager constantly asking people how things are going, the meeting that accomplishes little but morphs into another meeting next week, the cramped quarters into which people are crammed like sardines, the ringing phones of the sales department, or the loud lunchroom down the hall from your desk. These are the toxic by-products of offices these days.

Ever notice how much work you get done on a plane or a train? Or, however perversely, on vacation? Or when you hide in the basement? Or on a late Sunday afternoon when you have nothing else to do but crack open the laptop and pound some keys? It's in these moments—the moments far away from work, way outside the office—when it is the easiest to get work done. Interruption-free zones.

People aren't working longer and later because there's more work to do all of a sudden. People are working longer and later because they can't get work done at work anymore!

Office hours

We have all sorts of experts at Basecamp. People who can answer questions about statistics, JavaScript event handling, database tipping points, network diagnostics, and tricky copyediting. If you work here and you need an answer, all you have to do is ping the expert.

That's wonderful. And terrible.

It's wonderful when the right answer unlocks insight or progress. But it's terrible when that one expert is fielding their fifth random question of the day and suddenly the day is done.

The person with the question *needed* something and they got it. The person with the answer was *doing something else* and had to stop. That's rarely a fair trade.

The problem comes when you make it too easy—and always acceptable—to pose any question as soon as it comes to mind. Most questions just aren't that pressing, but the urge to ask the expert immediately is irresistible.

Now, if the sole reason they work there is to answer questions and be available for everyone else all day long, well, then, okay, sounds good. But our experts have their own work to do, too. You can't have both.

Imagine the day of an expert who frequently gets interrupted by everyone else's questions. They may be fielding none, a handful, or a dozen questions in a single day, who knows. What's worse, they don't know when these questions might come up. You can't plan your own day if everyone else is using it up randomly.

So we borrowed an idea from academia: office hours. All subject-matter experts at Basecamp now publish office hours. For some that means an open afternoon every Tuesday. For others it might be one hour a day. It's up to each expert to decide their availability.

But what if you have a question on Monday and someone's office hours aren't until Thursday? You wait, that's what you do. You work on something else until Thursday, or you figure it out for yourself before Thursday. Just like you would if you had to wait to talk to your professor.

This might seem inefficient at first glance. Bureaucratic, even. But we've seen otherwise. Office hours have been a big hit at Basecamp.

It turns out that waiting is no big deal most of the time. But the time and control regained by our experts is a huge deal. Calmer days, longer stretches of uninterrupted time to get things done, and planned moments when they can enter a more professorial mode and teach, help, and share.

It's something to look forward to and also something to put behind you. It's a great fit for everyone.

So keep the office door open (but only on Tuesdays from nine to noon!).

ALICE WATERS, THE CHEF WHO
PIONEERED THE SLOW FOOD
MOVEMENT, STARTS HER DAY
BY TAKING A WALK OR
MAKING A FIRE.

Calendar Tetris

The shared work calendar is one of the most destructive inventions of modern times. So much orbits around it, so much hinges on it, and so much is wrong because of it.

Getting on someone's schedule at Basecamp is a tedious, direct negotiation, not an easy, automated convenience. You have to make your case. You can't just reach into someone's calendar, find an open slot, and plant your flag. That's because no one can see anyone else's calendar at Basecamp.

This flies in the face of nearly every other company we've studied. In most places, everyone can see everyone else's day. People's calendars are not only completely transparent, they are optimized to be filled in by anyone who simply feels like it. Effectively, people are encouraged to slice other people's days into little 30-minute chunks of red, green, and blue appointment blocks.

Have you looked at your own calendar lately? How many things did you put there? How many things did other people put there?

When you optimize people's calendars for effortless carving, you shouldn't be surprised when people's time is sliced up. Furthermore, if you make it easy for someone to invite five other people to a meeting—because software can find the open slot that works for everyone—then meetings with six people will proliferate.

Taking someone's time should be a pain in the ass. Taking many people's time should be so cumbersome that most people won't even bother to try it unless it's REALLY IMPORTANT! Meetings should be a last resort, especially big ones.

When someone takes your time, it doesn't cost them anything, but it costs you everything. You can only do great work if you have adequate quality time to do it. So when someone takes that from you, they crush your feeling of accomplishment from a good day's work. The deep satisfaction you'd experience from actually making progress, not just talking about it, is eliminated.

If you don't own the vast majority of your own time, it's impossible to be calm. You'll always be stressed out, feeling robbed of the ability to actually do your job.

It's easy to excuse this game of calendar Tetris with "But it's just an invitation!" But nobody ever declines an invitation in good conscience. No one wants to be seen as "difficult" or "inaccessible." So they'll let the blocks drop until their day is crushed and the game is over.

If you can't be bothered to schedule a meeting without software to do the work, just don't bother at all. It probably wasn't necessary in the first place.

The presence prison

As a general rule, nobody at Basecamp really knows where anyone else is at any given moment. Are they working? Dunno. Are they taking a break? Dunno. Are they at lunch? Dunno. Are they picking up their kid from school? Dunno. Don't care.

We don't require anyone to broadcast their whereabouts or availability at Basecamp. No butts-in-seats requirement for people at the office, no virtual-status indicator when they're working remotely.

"But how do you know if someone's working if you can't see them?" Same answer as this question: "How do you know if someone's working if you *can* see them?" You don't. The only way to know if work is getting done is by looking at the actual work. That's the boss's job. If they can't do that job, they should find another one.

Technology has made the problem worse, too. Now it's not just the boss who wants to know where you are, it's everyone else, too. With the proliferation of chat tools invading the workplace, more and more people are being asked to broadcast their real-time status all the time. They're chained to the dot—green for available, red for away.

But when everyone knows you're "available," it's an invitation to be interrupted. You might as well have a neon sign flashing **BOTHER ME!** hanging above your head. Try being "available" for three hours and then try being "away" for three hours. Bet you get more work done when you're marked "away."

What if you need something from someone and you don't know whether they're available or not? Just ask them! If they respond, then you have what you needed. If they don't, it's not because they're ignoring you—it's because they're working on something else at the moment. Respect that! Assume people are focused on their own work.

Are there exceptions? Of course. It might be good to know who's around in a true emergency, but 1 percent occasions like that shouldn't drive policy 99 percent of the time.

So take a step toward calm, and relieve people from needing to broadcast their whereabouts and status. Everyone's status should be implicit: I'm trying to do my job, please respect my time and attention.

I'll get back to you whenever

The expectation of an immediate response is the ember that ignites so many fires at work.

First someone emails you. Then if they don't hear from you in a few minutes, they text you. No answer? Next they call you. Then they ask someone else where you are. And that someone else goes through the same steps to get your attention.

All of a sudden you're pulled away from what you're working on. And why? Is it a crisis? Okay, fine then! They're excused. But if it's not—and it almost never is—then there's no excuse.

In almost every situation, the expectation of an immediate response is an unreasonable expectation. Yet with more and more real-time communication tools creeping into daily work—especially instant-messaging tools and group chat—the expectation of an immediate response has become the new normal.

This is not progress.

The common thinking goes like this: If I can write you quickly, you can get back to me quickly, right? Technically, right. Practically, wrong.

How fast you can reach someone has nothing to do with how quickly they need to get back to you. The content of the communication dictates that. Emergencies? Okay. You need me to resend that thing I sent you last week? That can wait. You need an answer to a question you can find yourself? That can wait. You need to know what time the client's coming in three days from now? That can wait.

Almost everything can wait. And almost everything should.

At Basecamp, we've tried to create a culture of eventual response rather than immediate response. One where everyone doesn't lose their shit if the answer to a nonurgent question arrives three hours later. One where we not only accept but strongly encourage people not to check email, or chat, or instant message for long stretches of uninterrupted time.

Give it a try. Say something, then get back to work. Don't expect anything. You'll get a response when the other person is free and ready to respond.

And if someone doesn't get back to you quickly, it's not because they're ignoring you—it's probably because they're working. Don't you have some other work to do while you wait?

Waiting it out is just fine. The sky won't fall, the company won't fold. It'll just be a calmer, cooler, more comfortable place to work. For everyone.

FOMO? JOMO!

FOMO. The fear of missing out. It's the affliction that drives obsessive checking of Twitter feeds, Facebook updates, Instagram stories, WhatsApp groups, and news apps. It's not uncommon for people to pick up their phones dozens of times a day when some push notification makes it buzz, because WHAT IF IT WAS SOMETHING SUPER IMPORTANT! (It just about never is.)

And it's no longer contained to social media—it's seeping into work as well. As if email wasn't bad enough at cultivating FOMO, we now have a new generation of real-time tools like chat to stoke it. Yet another thing that asks for your continuous partial attention all day on the premise that you can't miss out.

Fuck that. People should be missing out! Most people should miss out on most things most of the time. That's what we try to encourage at Basecamp. JOMO! The joy of missing out.

It's JOMO that lets you turn off the firehose of information and chatter and interruptions to actually get the right shit done. It's JOMO that lets you catch up on what happened today as a single summary email tomorrow morning rather than with a drip-drip-drip feed throughout the day. JOMO, baby, JOMO.

Because there's absolutely no reason everyone needs to attempt to know everything that's going on at our company. And especially not in real time! If it's important, you'll find out. And most of it isn't. Most of the day-to-day work inside a company's walls is mundane. And that's a beautiful thing. It's work, it's not news. We must all stop treating every little fucking thing that happens at work like it's on a breaking-news ticker.

One way we push back against this at Basecamp is by writing monthly "Heartbeats." Summaries of the work and progress that's been done and had by a team, written by the team lead, to the entire company. All the minutiae boiled down to the essential points others would care to know. Just enough to keep someone in the loop without having to internalize dozens of details that don't matter.

At many companies these days, people treat every detail at work like there's going to be a pop quiz. They have to know every fact, every figure, every name, every event. This is a waste of brain power and an even more egregious waste of attention.

Focus on your work at hand. That's all we ask. That's all we require. If there's anything you must know, we promise you'll hear about it. If you're curious, cool—follow whatever you want—but we want people to feel the oblivious joy of focus rather than the frantic, manic fear of missing something that didn't matter anyway.

THE PHYSICIST STEPHEN HAWKING TOOK A LONG VIEW OF RESEARCH AND WORK, ENCOURAGING HIS STUDENTS TO SPEND TIME ON OTHER ACTIVITIES LIKE LISTENING TO MUSIC AND SOCIALIZING WITH FRIENDS.

Feed Your Culture

We're not family

Companies love to declare "We're all family here." No, you're not. Neither are we at Basecamp. We're coworkers. That doesn't mean we don't care about one another. That doesn't mean we won't go out of our way for one another. We do care and we do help. But a family we are not. And neither is your business.

Furthermore, Basecamp is not "our baby." Basecamp is our product. We'll make it great, but we won't take a bullet for it. And neither would you for yours.

We don't need to bullshit ourselves or anyone else. We're people who work together to make a product. And we're proud of it. That's enough.

Whenever executives talk about how their company is really like a big ol' family, beware. They're usually not referring to how the company is going to protect you no matter what or love you unconditionally. You know, like healthy families would. Their motive is rather more likely to be a unidirectional form of sacrifice: yours.

Because by invoking the image of the family, the valor of doing whatever it takes naturally follows. You're not just working long nights or skipping a vacation to further the bottom line; no, no, you're doing this *for the family*. Such a blunt emotional appeal is only needed if someone is trying to make you forget about your rational self-interest.

You don't have to pretend to be a family to be courteous. Or kind. Or protective. All those values can be expressed even better in principles, policies, and, most important, actions.

Besides, don't you already have a family or group of friends who feel like blood? The modern company isn't a street gang filled with orphans trying to make it in the tough, tough world. Trying to supplant the family you likely already have is just another way to attempt to put the needs of the company above the needs of your actual family. That's a sick ploy.

The best companies aren't families. They're supporters of families. Allies of families. They're there to provide healthy, fulfilling work environments so that when workers shut their laptops at a reasonable hour, they're the best husbands, wives, parents, siblings, and children they can be.

They'll do as you do

You can't credibly promote the virtues of reasonable hours, plentiful rest, and a healthy lifestyle to employees if you're doing the opposite as the boss. When the top dog puts in mad hours, the rest of the pack is bound to follow along. It doesn't matter what you say, it matters what you do.

It gets even worse in a business with layers. If your manager's manager is setting a bad example, that impression rolls down the hierarchy and gathers momentum like a snowball.

Take those trite stories about the CEO who only sleeps four hours each night, is the first in the parking lot, has three meetings before breakfast, and turns out the light after midnight. What a hero! Truly someone who lives and breathes the company before themselves!

No, not a hero. If the only way you can inspire the troops is by a regimen of exhaustion, it's time to look for some deeper substance. Because what trickles down is less likely to be admiration but dread and fear instead. A leader who sets an example of self-sacrifice can't help but ask self-sacrifice of others.

Maybe that's a valiant quality on the battlefield, but it's hardly one in the office. The fate of most companies is not decided in fierce contests of WHO CAN DO THE LATEST CONFERENCE CALL or WHO CAN SET THE MOST PUNISHING DEADLINE.

If you, as the boss, want employees to take vacations, you have to take a vacation. If you want them to stay home when they're sick, you can't come into the office sniffling. If you don't want them to feel guilty for taking their kids to Legoland on the weekend, post some pictures of yourself there with yours.

Workaholism is a contagious disease. You can't stop the spread if you're the one bringing it into the office. Disseminate some calm instead.

The trust battery

Ever been in a relationship where you're endlessly annoyed by every little thing the other person does? In isolation, the irritating things aren't objectively annoying. But in those cases it's never really about the little things. There's something else going on.

The same thing can happen at work. Someone says something, or acts in a certain way, and someone else blows up about it. From afar it looks like an overreaction. You can't figure out what the big deal is. There's something else going on.

Here's what's going on: The trust battery is dead.

Tobias Lütke, CEO at Shopify, coined the term. Here's how he explained it in a *New York Times* interview: "Another concept we talk a lot about is something called a 'trust battery.' It's charged at 50 percent when people are first hired. And then every time you work with someone at the company, the trust battery between the two of you is either charged or discharged, based on things like whether you deliver on what you promise."

The adoption of this term at Basecamp helped us assess work relationships with greater clarity. It removed the natural instinct to evaluate whether someone is "right" about their feelings about another person (which is a nonsense concept to begin with). By measuring the charge on the trust battery, we have context to frame the conflict.

The reality is that the trust battery is a summary of all interactions to date. If you want to recharge the battery, you have to do different things in the future. Only new actions and new attitudes count.

Plus, it's personal. Alice's trust battery with Bob is different from Carol's trust battery with Bob. Bob may be at 85 percent with Alice but only 10 percent with Carol. Bob isn't going to recharge his battery with Carol just by acting differently with Alice. The work of recharging relationships is mostly one to one. That's why two people who get along often can't understand how someone else could have a problem with their good friend.

A low trust battery is at the core of many personal disputes at work. It powers stressful encounters and anxious moments. When the battery is drained, everything is wrong, everything is judged harshly. A 10 percent charge equals a 90 percent chance an interaction will go south.

Having good relationships at work takes, err, *work*. The kind that can only begin once you're honest about where you're starting from. The worst thing you can do is pretend that interpersonal feelings don't matter. That work should "just be about work." That's just ignorant. Humans are humans whether they're at work or at home.

Don't be the last to know

When the boss says "My door is always open," it's a cop-out, not an invitation. One that puts the onus of speaking up entirely on the employees.

The only time such an empty gesture serves any purpose is after the shit has already hit the fan. Then it can be dragged out of the drawer with "Why didn't you just come and tell me?" and "I told you if you ever had an issue with anything that you should come talk to me." *eyeroll*

What the boss most needs to hear is where they and the organization are falling short. But who knows how a superior is going to take such pointed feedback? It's a minefield, and every employee knows someone who's been blown up for raising the wrong issue at the wrong time to the wrong boss. Why on earth would they risk their career on an empty promise of an open door?

They generally won't, and they shouldn't have to.

If the boss really wants to know what's going on, the answer is embarrassingly obvious: They have to ask! Not vague, self-congratulatory bullshit questions like "What can we do even better?" but the hard ones like "What's something nobody dares to talk about?" or "Are you afraid of anything at work?" or "Is there anything you worked on recently that you wish you could do over?" Or even more specific ones like "What do you think we could have done differently to help Jane succeed?" or "What advice would you give before we start on the big website redesign project?"

Posing real, pointed questions is the only way to convey that it's safe to provide real answers. And even then it's going to take a while. Maybe you get 20 percent of the story the first time you ask, then 50 percent after a while, and if you've really nailed it as a trustworthy boss, you may get to 80 percent. Forget about ever getting the whole story.

The fact is that the higher you go in an organization, the less you'll know what it's *really* like. It might seem perverse, but the CEO is usually the last to know. With great power comes great ignorance.

So at Basecamp we try to get out and ask rather than just wait at the door. Not all the time, because you shouldn't ask before you're willing and able to act on the answer, but often enough to know most of what's going on most of the time.

BRUNO CUCINELLI, FOUNDER OF THE EPONYMOUS ITALIAN FASHION BRAND, FORBIDS HIS EMPLOYEES FROM WORKING PAST 5:30 PM BECAUSE HE BELIEVES SENDING EMAIL AFTER BUSINESS HOURS INTRUDES INTO THEIR PRIVATE LIVES.

The owner's word
weighs a ton

There's no such thing as a casual suggestion when it comes from the owner of the business. When the person who signs the paychecks mentions this or that, this or that invariably becomes a top priority.

So something as minor as "Are we doing enough on Instagram?" can shoot Instagram to the top of the marketing priority list. It was a mere suggestion, but it's taken as a mandate. "Why would she be talking about Instagram unless she really thought Instagram was super important?"

It only gets worse if employees find the owner pulling at the weeds themselves. If the boss is looking over there, then clearly we should all be looking over there! They might just have been curious or looking for something to do, but that's not the impression it makes.

An owner unknowingly scattering people's attention is a common cause of the question "Why's everyone working so much but nothing's getting done?"

It takes great restraint as the leader of an organization not to keep lobbing ideas at everyone else. Every such idea is a pebble that's going to cause ripples when it hits the surface. Throw enough pebbles in the pond and the overall picture becomes as clear as mud.

Evading responsibility with a "But it's just a suggestion" isn't going to calm the waters. Only knowing the weight of the owner's word will.

Low-hanging fruit can still be out of reach

You've probably said or heard something like this before:

"We've never had anyone in business development, so there must be a ton of low-hanging fruit she can go after with just a little bit of effort."

"We've never done any social media outreach, so imagine how much new traffic"—low-hanging fruit—"we'll get if we just start tweeting stuff out."

"We've never followed up with customers who cancel to better understand why they left, so I'm certain there's plenty of low-hanging fruit to be had if we do those interviews."

We're definitely guilty of having thought about things in these terms. By definition, pursuing low-hanging fruit should be a no-brainer for any business. An easy opportunity simply waiting to be seized. Little sweat, all reward!

The problem, as we've learned over time, is that the further away you are from the fruit, the lower it looks. Once you get up close, you see it's quite a bit higher than you thought. We assume that picking it will be easy only because we've never tried to do it before.

Declaring that an unfamiliar task will yield low-hanging fruit is almost always an admission that you have little insight about what you're setting out to do. And any estimate of how much work it'll take to do something you've never tried before is likely to be off by degrees of magnitude.

The worst is when you load up these expectations on new hires and assume they'll meet them all quickly. You're basically setting them up to fail.

We recently found ourselves in this very position. We hired someone to run business development at Basecamp for the first time. We figured they'd make a few calls and quickly line up a few partnerships, and then we'd see the results pour in. Since we'd never had anyone focus on this area previously, we counted on there being a load of treasure just inches beneath the surface. How hard could it be, right? Turns out, we've had to do quite a lot more digging than we realized to unearth the gold. In fact, we've stopped looking.

The same thing happened when we decided to start sending a few more follow-up emails after someone signs up for Basecamp to increase conversions of trial users into paying customers. Previously, we had been sending users a single email when they signed up and nothing much after that. So we imagined that sending more emails over time would quickly move the conversion numbers north.

It didn't. What looked like low-hanging fruit was neither ripe nor within reach.

The idea that you'll instantly move needles because you've never tried to move them until now is, well, delusional. Sometimes you get lucky and things are as easy as you had imagined, but that's rarely the case. Most conversion work, most business-development work, most sales work is a grind—a lot of effort for a little movement. You pile those little movements into a big one eventually, but that fruit is way up at the top of the tree.

So the next time you ask an employee to go pick some low-hanging fruit—stop yourself. Respect the work that you've never done before. Remind yourself that other people's jobs aren't so simple. Results rarely come without effort. If momentum and experience are on your side, what is hard can masquerade as easy, but never forget that not having done something before doesn't make it easy. It usually makes it hard.

Don't cheat sleep

Sleep is for the weak! Real A players only need four to five hours! Great accomplishments require great sacrifice!

Bull. Shit.

The people who brag about trading sleep for endless slogs and midnight marathons are usually the ones who can't point to actual accomplishments. Telling tales of endless slogs is a diversionary tactic. It's pathetic.

It's not worth trading sleep for a few extra hours at the office. Not only will it make you exhausted, it'll literally make you stupid. The science is clear on this: Continued sleep deprivation batters your IQ and saps your creativity. You may be too tired to notice, but the people you work with will.

Yet somehow it's still frequently seen as heroic to sacrifice yourself, your health, and even your ability to do your job just to prove your loyalty to THE MISSION. Fuck the mission. No mission (in business, anyway) is worthy of such dire personal straits.

Sleep-deprived people aren't just short on brains or creativity, they're short on patience. Short on understanding. Short on tolerance. The smallest things become the biggest dramas. That hurts colleagues at work as much as it does the family at home. Being short on sleep turns the astute into assholes.

The effects multiply for those directly responsible for others. Managers need double the empathy, not half a ration. If they're worn thin, their short fuse quickly becomes the baseline for the team. Even well-rested individuals can get caught up in a storm of nonsense if it's started by their superior.

Besides, if the point of all those long hours is to get more done, shouldn't you at least actually, you know, get more done? Ask anyone who's been on a two-week bender with little sleep if they can remember what they did last Tuesday. Most probably cannot. And no, "lots of stuff" doesn't count.

Yes, sometimes you can do a quick sprint. Or burn a drop of the midnight oil just to get over the hump. But, man, is that a fine line cut with a thin razor.

Because what happens over and over again is that people who start on long hours simply stay on long hours. We're all creatures of habit. Breaking the cycle once it's been internalized might well require a full bout of rehab, if not an outright intervention. Be careful taking that first hit!

Better yet, just skip out on cheating sleep. Get a good eight hours every night, even when you're first getting started. Those hours will not be wasted. A great night's sleep enhances every waking hour. Isn't that what you're looking for anyway?

Remember, your brain is still active at night. It works through matters you can't address during the day. Don't you want to wake up with new solutions in your head rather than bags under your eyes?

Yes, sometimes emergencies require extra hours. And yes, sometimes deadlines can't be moved and you'll need to make an extra push at the end. That happens. And that's okay because the exhaustion is not sustained, it's temporary.

In the long run, work is not more important than sleep.

Very few problems need to be solved at the twelfth or fifteenth hour of a workday. All-nighters are red flags, not green lights. If people are pulling them, pull back. Nearly everything can wait until morning.

Out of whack

At most companies, work-life balance is a sham. Not because there shouldn't be a balance, but because work always seems to end up putting its fat finger on the scale. Life just lifts. That's not balance.

Balance is give and take. The typical corporate give-and-take is that life gives and work takes. If it's easier for work to claim a Sunday than for life to borrow a Thursday, there ain't no balance.

With seven days in a week, and work already owning the majority of your waking hours for at least five of them, life already starts at a disadvantage. And that's okay—something has to pay for living. But that five is already plenty.

It's pretty basic. If you work Monday to Friday, weekends should be off-limits for work.

And it's also why if you decide you want to take a Wednesday to hang with your kids, that's cool, too. You don't have to "make up" the day—just be responsible with your time and make sure your team knows when you won't be around. It all rounds out in the end.

The same thing is true with weekday nights. If work can claim hours after 5:00 p.m., then life should be able to claim hours before 5:00 p.m. Balance, remember. Give and take.

We ask reasonable people to make reasonable choices, and the company will be reasonable right back. That's balance.

TELEVISION PRODUCER AND
SCREENWRITER SHONDA RHIMES
RUNS MULTIPLE PRIMETIME
SHOWS WHILE STICKING TO A
POLICY OF NOT ANSWERING
PHONE CALLS OR RETURNING
EMAILS AFTER 7PM AND
DURING WEEKENDS.

Hire the work, not the résumé

Few things in business are as stressful as realizing you hired the wrong person. And it doesn't end there because now what? Now you'll either have to let them go (stressful for you and them) or tolerate the bad fit (stressful for you, them, and everyone else on the team). One stress breeds another stress.

And sometimes it's more subtle than that. Someone may be the right individual fit, but they may not fit the team. Whenever someone joins (or leaves) a team, the old team is gone. It's a new team now. No matter the group, every personnel change changes the dynamics.

While it's impossible to hire perfectly, you can certainly increase your odds if you reconsider your approach toward evaluating candidates.

Here's how we do it.

First, you can't land a job at Basecamp based on your résumé. CVs might as well be tossed in the garbage. We don't really care where you went to school, or how many years you've been working in the industry, or even that much about where you just worked. What we care about is who you are and what you can do.

So you have to be good people. Someone the rest of the team *wants* to work with, not just someone they'd tolerate. It doesn't matter how good you are at the job if you're an ass. Nothing you can do for us would make up for that.

But it's even more than that. We look for candidates who are interesting and different from the people we already have. We don't need 50 twentysomething clones in hoodies with all of the same cultural references. We do better work, broader work, and more considered work when the team reflects the diversity of our customer base. "Not exactly what we already have" is a quality in itself.

If the candidate clears that bar—being someone people are excited to work with and who can bring a new perspective to the table—then it's all about the work. Résumés aren't work. Résumés may list the work they've done, but we all know that they are exaggerated and often bullshit. Beyond that—even if their résumé is perfectly accurate—a list of work is not the work itself. Don't just take their word for it. Take their work for it.

Yes, maybe you were a designer on the nike.com redesign, but what part of it did you do? A résumé can't usually answer that question. And since a lot of the work people do at their previous jobs is proprietary, hard to pin down, with a team of people, or ambiguous at best, at Basecamp we put a real project in front of the candidates so that they can *show* us what *they* can do.

For example, when we're choosing a new designer, we hire each of the finalists for a week, pay them $1,500 for that time, and ask them to do a sample project for us. Then we have something to evaluate that's current, real, and completely theirs.

What we don't do are riddles, blackboard problem solving, or fake "come up with the answer on the spot" scenarios. We don't answer riddles all day, we do real work. So we give people real work to do and the appropriate time to do it in. It's the same kind of work they'd be doing if they got the job.

The idea here is that by focusing on the person and their work, we can avoid hiring an imaginary person. It's really easy to fall for someone's carefully crafted story. Great pedigree, great school, impressive list of previous employment. What's not to love? This is how companies hire the wrong people all the time. They hire someone based on a list of previous qualifications, not on their current abilities.

When you force yourself to focus on just the person and their work, not their glorified past, you also end up giving more people a chance. There's no GPA filter to cut out someone who didn't care for certain parts of their schooling. There's no pedigree screen to prevent the self-taught from getting hired. There's no arbitrary "years of experience" cut to prevent a fast learner from applying to a senior position.

Great people who are eager to do great work come from the most unlikely places and look nothing like what you might imagine. Focusing just on the person and their work is the only way to spot them.

Nobody hits the
ground running

"We just want someone who can hit the ground running" is the common refrain for companies seeking senior-level job candidates. There's a natural assumption that someone who was already, say, a lead programmer or designer in their previous job will be able to step right into that role anywhere and be effective immediately. That just isn't so. Organizations differ widely. The skills and experience needed to get traction in one place are often totally different somewhere else.

Take managerial direction, for example. At Basecamp, we've designed the organization to be largely manager-free. This means people are generally responsible for setting their own short- to medium-term direction and will only get top-level directives.

That can be an uncomfortable setup when someone is used to having more hands-on, day-to-day direction about what to work on. The more accustomed someone is to that kind of directed form of work, the more they'll have to unlearn. That kind of unlearning can be just as hard as having to pick up entirely new skills—and sometimes even harder.

The same is true if they're the kind of senior person who's used to getting stuff done mainly by directing others to do it. At Basecamp, we all do the work, so influence is most effectively exerted by leading the work, not by calling for it.

All these dangers are multiplied when you have senior people who switch from a role at a big company to a little company or vice versa. It's especially tempting to think that if you work in a small company, you could really benefit from someone with the experience from a big company to help you "grow up." But trying to teach a small company how to act like a big one rarely does anyone any good. You're usually better off finding someone who's familiar with the challenges at your company's size or thereabouts.

The fact is that unless you hire someone straight out of an identical role at an identical company, they're highly unlikely to be instantly up to speed and able to deliver right away. That doesn't mean that a particular opening might not be the best fit for a senior-level person, but the decision shouldn't be based on the misconception of immediate results.

The quickest way to disappointment is to set unreasonable expectations.

Ignore the talent war

Talent isn't worth fighting over. It's not a fixed, scarce resource that either you have or you don't. It rarely even transplants all that well. Someone who's a superstar at one company often turns out to be completely ineffectual at another. Don't go to war over talent.

In fact, junk the whole metaphor of talent wars altogether. Stop thinking of talent as something to be plundered and start thinking of it as something to be grown and nurtured, the seeds for which are readily available all over the globe for companies willing to do the work.

That work is mostly about the environment, anyway. Even if you had the most precious orchid planted in your garden, it would quickly die without the proper care. And if you do pay attention to having the best environment, you can grow your own beautiful orchids with patience. No need to steal them from your neighbor!

At Basecamp, you're not going to find any high-profile super-stars that we lured away from other companies. But you'll find plenty of talented people, most of whom have been with the company for many years and in some cases for more than a decade.

Pretty much none of the talent came from the traditional war zones in our industry, like San Francisco, the larger Bay Area, or even Seattle or New York. Not because there aren't a lot of great people there, but because there are a lot of great people everywhere.

For example, we found a wonderful designer in Oklahoma working for a newspaper, an awesome programmer in the rural outskirts of Toronto working at a small web design shop, and an outstanding customer service person in Tennessee working in a deli. On top of not considering provenance or location, we don't consider formal education, either. We look at people's actual work, not at their diploma or degree.

We've found that nurturing untapped potential is far more exhilarating than finding someone who's already at their peak. We hired many of our best people not because of who they were but because of who they could become.

It takes patience to grow and nurture your own talent. But the work it takes—tending to the calm-culture soil—is the same work that improves the company for everyone. Get to it.

Don't negotiate salaries

To be paid fairly at most companies, it's not enough to just be really good at your job. You also have to be an ace negotiator. Most people aren't, so they end up getting shortchanged—sometimes making less money than more junior peers who were recently hired.

The thing is, most people just don't enjoy haggling, period. Not for a car, not for a house, not for their livelihood. It's an unpleasant situation, and even if you do it well, you can easily end up with a lingering dread of "I wonder if I could have gotten more?!" (That feeling often kicks in if your offer is quickly accepted!)

So why do companies subject everyone to such a lame game year after year?

Well, we did it for years, too. It's just one of those things that seem to be an immutable law of business. But it isn't, and a few years ago we took a detour and made a decision to eliminate the stress that goes along with the annual salary-renegotiation ritual entirely.

We no longer negotiate salaries or raises at Basecamp. Everyone in the same role at the same level is paid the same. Equal work, equal pay.

We assess new hires on a scale that goes from junior programmer, to programmer, to senior programmer, to lead programmer, to principal programmer (or designer or customer support or ops or whatever role we're hiring for). We use the same scale to assess when someone is in line for a promotion. Every employee, new or old, fits into a level on the scale, and there is a salary pegged to each level per role.

Once every year we review market rates and issue raises automatically. Our target is to pay everyone at the company at the top 10 percent of the market regardless of their role. So whether you work in customer support or ops or programming or design, you'll be paid in the top 10 percent for that position.

If someone is below that target, they get a raise large enough to match the target. If someone is already above the target, they stay where they are. (We're not going to cut the pay for existing employees if the market dips for their role.) If someone is promoted, they get a raise to match the market rate for the new level.

We get the market rates through a variety of salary survey companies. They poll a wide array of companies in our industry (from the titans to shops more comparable in size to Basecamp). It's not a perfect system, and we do frequently cross-check with other sources, but it's certainly better than going by a few "I've heard that X pays Y . . ."

Our market rates are based on San Francisco numbers despite the fact that we don't have a single employee there. San Francisco is simply the highest-paying city in the world for our industry. So no matter where you choose to live, we pay the same top-market salaries. After all, where you live has nothing to do with the quality of your work, and it's the quality of your work that we're paying you for. What difference does it make that your bed is in Boston, Barcelona, or Bangladesh?

We didn't start out paying everyone these extremely high San Francisco salaries. For a while we were following a similar model but using Chicago rates. The important part isn't really whether you can afford to pay salaries based on the top city in your industry or at the top 10 percent of the market, but that you keep salaries equal for equal work and seniority.

This gives everyone at the company the freedom to pick where they want to live, and there's no penalty for relocating to a cheaper cost-of-living area. We encourage remote work and have many employees who've lived all over the world while continuing to work for Basecamp.

We don't pay traditional bonuses at Basecamp, either, so our salaries are benchmarked against other companies' salaries plus bonus packages. (We used to do bonuses many years ago, but we found that they were quickly treated as expected salary, anyway. So if they ever dipped, people felt like they got a demotion.)

There are no stock options at Basecamp because we never intend to sell the company. Besides, if you've worked somewhere where stock options are a healthy percentage of compensation, you know the stress a volatile market can cause. Not exactly a conductor of calm.

So here's what we do instead: We've vowed to distribute 5 percent of the proceeds to all current employees if we ever sell the company. No stock price to follow, no valuation to worry about. If something happens, we'll share. If not, no need to spend any time thinking about it. It's a pleasant surprise, it's not compensation.

We've also recently put a new profit growth-sharing scheme in place. If total profits grow year over year, we'll distribute 25 percent of that growth to employees in that year. This isn't tied to role, it's not about individual performance, and since we don't have salespeople, it's not commission. Everyone shares or no one gets it.

There are surely a few places where people can get paid more than they can at Basecamp. Especially if they're pro negotiators and able to persuade an employer to pay them more than their peers for the same work.

There are also plenty of places that'll offer "lottery tickets" (aka stock options) that could make someone an overnight millionaire if they join a startup that eventually, against all odds, turns into the next Google or Facebook.

But Basecamp isn't a startup. We've been in our current business as a software company since 2004. It's a stable, sustainable, and profitable enterprise.

No compensation system is perfect, but at least under this model, nobody is forced to hop jobs just to get a raise that matches their market value. These results are reflected in the fact that we have lots of people at Basecamp who've been here for a long time with no plans to leave. At the time of publication of this book, a notch over 50 percent of our employees have been here for five years or more. That's rarefied air in an industry where the average tenure at the top tech companies is less than two years.

Of course, pay isn't the only reason someone might leave our company. We've had people leave Basecamp for a number of reasons. For example, they wanted to give the Silicon Valley lottery a try or they wanted a completely different career. That's healthy! Some amount of turnover is a good thing, but salary shouldn't be the main driver for most people.

Hiring and training people is not only expensive, but draining. All that energy could go into making better products with people you've kept happy for the long term by being fair and transparent about salary and benefits. Churning through people because you're trying to suppress the wages of those who stay just seems like poor business.

There's a fountain of happiness and productivity in working with a stable crew. It's absolutely key to how we're able to do so much with so few at Basecamp. We're baffled that such a competitive advantage isn't more diligently sought.

PATAGONIA FOUNDER
YVON CHOUINARD
SPENDS PART OF THE YEAR
IN WYOMING, WHERE HE HIKES,
FLY FISHES, AND CHECKS IN
WITH THE OFFICE JUST
TWICE A WEEK.

Benefits who?

Have you heard about those companies whose benefits include game-console rooms, cereal snack bars, top-chef lunches and dinners, nap rooms, laundry service, and free beer on Fridays? It seems so generous, but there's also a catch: You can't leave the office.

These fancy benefits blur the lines between work and play to the point where it's mostly just work. When you look at it like that, it isn't really generous—it's insidious.

Consider the free dinner for employees who stay late. How is staying late a benefit? Or those free lunches that often just end up cutting into break time and keeping workers on campus versus down the street. Talk about putting the "there's no free lunch" in "free lunch."

There's an uncanny correlation between the companies with these kinds of benefits and the companies that can't stop talking about the need to push work to the max. Dinners, lunches, game rooms, late nights—these mainly exist at companies that work 60-plus hours a week, not 40. Sounds more like bribes than benefits, doesn't it?

At Basecamp, we're having none of that. Not just because we don't require anyone to physically come to our office to work, but because we don't offer gotcha benefits. There's no mission to maximize the hours we make employees stay at the office. We aren't looking to get the most out of everyone, we're only looking for what's reasonable. That requires balance.

That's why we look at benefits as a way to help people get away from work and lead healthier, more interesting lives. Benefits that actually benefit *them*, not the company. Although the company clearly benefits, too, from having healthier, more interesting, well-rested workers.

Here's a list of relevant "outside the office" benefits we offer all employees, regardless of position, regardless of salary:

- Fully paid vacations every year for everyone who's been with the company for more than a year. Not just the time off, but we'll actually pay for the whole trip—airfare, hotel accommodations—up to $5,000 per person or family.
- Three-day weekends all summer. May through September we only work 32-hour weeks. This allows everyone to take Friday off, or Monday off, so they can have a full three-day weekend, every weekend, all summer long.

- 30-day-paid sabbaticals every three years. People can spend it at home doing nothing, deep-diving into a new skill, or hiking the Himalayas. Whatever floats their boat.
- $1,000 per year continuing-education stipend. This isn't about learning a skill people can use at work—it's about everything outside of work. Want to learn how to play the banjo? It's on us. Want to learn how to cook? It's on us. None of these things have anything to do with work at Basecamp—they all have to do with encouraging people to do things they've always wanted to do but needed a bit of encouragement and help to actually make happen.
- $2,000 per year charity match. Donate to a charity of your choice up to $2,000, and we'll match it up to $2,000.
- A local monthly CSA (community-supported agriculture) share. This means fresh fruits and vegetables at *home* for people and their families.
- One monthly massage at an actual spa, not the office.
- $100 monthly fitness allowance. We'll basically pay for people's health club membership, yoga classes, running shoes, race registrations, or whatever else they do to stay healthy on a regular basis.

Not a single benefit aimed at trapping people at the office. Not a single benefit that would make someone prefer to be at work rather than at home. Not a single benefit that puts work ahead of life. Instead, plenty of reasons to close the laptop at a reasonable time so that there's time to learn, cook, work out, and live life with family and friends.

Library rules

Whoever managed to rebrand the typical open-plan office—with all its noise, lack of privacy, and resulting interruptions—as something hip and modern deserves a damn medal from the Committee of Irritating Distractions. Such offices are great at one thing: packing in as many people as possible at the expense of the individual.

Open-plan offices suck at providing an environment for calm, creative work done by professionals who need peace, quiet, privacy, and space to think and do their best.

It's even worse when you mix professions with different requirements. When sales or service people, who often need to be loud and jovial on the phone, have to share accommodations with people who need long stretches of quiet, you're not only destroying productivity, you're fomenting resentment.

In spaces like that, distractions spread like viruses. Before you know it, everyone's infected.

While closed, private individual offices are one reasonable solution, if everyone doesn't get one you'll be breeding bitterness. But there's good news: You don't have to give up on the open-plan office per se, but you do need to give up on the typical open-office mindset.

That's what we did with our Chicago office at Basecamp. Rather than thinking of it as an office, we think of it as a library. In fact, we call our guiding principle: Library Rules.

Walk into a library anywhere in the world and you'll notice the same thing: It's quiet and calm. Everyone knows how to behave in a library. In fact, few things transcend cultures like library behavior. It's a place where people go to read, think, study, focus, and work. And the hushed, respectful environment reflects that.

Isn't that what an office should be?

People who visit our office for the first time are startled by the silence and serenity. It doesn't look, sound, or behave like a traditional office. That's because it's really a library for work rather than an office for distraction.

In our office, if someone's at their desk, we assume they're deep in thought and focused on their work. That means we don't walk up to them and interrupt them. It also means conversations should be kept to a whisper so as not to disturb anyone who could possibly hear you. Quiet runs the show.

To account for the need for the occasional full-volume collaboration, we've designated a handful of small rooms in the center of the office where people can go to if they need to work on something together (or make a private call).

A few simple choices, a shift in mindset, and a cultural respect for everyone's time, attention, focus, and work are all that's necessary to make Library Rules your rules. People already instinctively know Library Rules, they just need to practice them at the office, too.

Skeptical? Make the first Thursday of the month Library Rules day at the office. We bet your employees will beg for more.

No fakecations

When someone takes a vacation at Basecamp, it should feel like
they don't work here anymore. We encourage them to go completely dark: Log out of Basecamp on their computer, delete the
Basecamp app from their phone, and don't check in. Go away
for real. Be gone. Off our grid.

The whole purpose of a vacation is to get away. To not only be
somewhere else entirely, but to think about something else entirely. Work should not be on your mind. Period.

But the reality is that most companies don't actually offer their
employees any real vacation time. All they offer is a "fakeca-
tion" where employees can still be reeled into conference calls,
asked to "hop on a quick call about something," or expected to
be available whenever a question comes up.

If you work full-time, when was the last time you actually got to
disconnect full-time? Not for a weekend, but for weeks. When
you didn't hear from coworkers while away. When you didn't
feel any guilt or urge to check in and check up on work. Far too

few people, especially in the United States, can claim such a thing nowadays. That's a tragedy.

Fakecations put employees on a leash—liable to be yanked back and pulled into work at any moment. Time off isn't much of a benefit if it can be taken right back. That's more like a shitty loan with terrible terms. Plus interest. And worries. Screw that.

Employers aren't entitled to anyone's nights, weekends, or vacations. That's life time. True emergencies are an exception, but those should only happen once or twice a year max.

When companies act like they own all of their employees' time, they breed a culture of neurotic exhaustion. Everyone needs a chance to truly get away and reboot. If they're denied that, especially during sanctioned vacation time, they're going to return tired and resentful.

And don't try to justify fakecations by saying "But you can take as much as you want!" In our industry, it's become common practice to offer "unlimited vacation days." It sounds so appealing! But peel back the label and it's a pretty rotten practice.

Unlimited vacation is a stressful benefit because it's not truly unlimited. Can someone really take five months off? No. Three? No. Two? One? Maybe? Is it weeks or months? Who's to know for sure? Ambiguity breeds anxiety.

We learned this the hard way. At one point we tried offering unlimited vacation, but we eventually noticed that people actually ended up taking less time off than they otherwise should have! That was exactly the opposite of what we intended.

Nobody wants to be seen as a slacker. Or overstay a seemingly generous policy. So they all err on the safe side, which ends up being not very much at all. They take their cues from whoever is taking the least vacation on the team already.

So here's our official policy today: "Basecamp offers three weeks of paid vacation, a few extra personal days to use at your discretion, and the standard national holidays every year. This is a guideline, so if you need a couple extra days, no problem. We don't track your days off, we use the honor system. Just make sure to check with your team before taking any extended absence, so they're not left in the lurch."

Three weeks is clear, but personal discretion is still there if you need a little more. Just be mindful of the impact, let your team know, then unplug entirely and have a great vacation. The world will still be standing when you return.

Calm goodbyes

While the act of letting someone go is unpleasant for all in-volved, it's a moment in time. It passes. What remains after the dismissal are all the great folks who still work at the company. People who will be curious about what happened to their co-worker. Why aren't they here anymore? Who's next? If I don't know, could it be me?

At many companies, when someone's let go, all you get are vague euphemisms. "Hey, what happened to Bob?" "Oh, Bob? We don't talk about Bob anymore. It was simply time for him to move on." Fuck that.

If you don't clearly communicate to everyone else why someone was let go, the people who remain at the company will come up with their own story to explain it. Those stories will almost certainly be worse than the real reason.

A dismissal opens a vacuum, and unless you fill that vacuum with facts, it'll quickly fill with rumors, conjecture, anxiety, and fear. If you want to avoid that, you simply have to be hon-est and clear with everyone about what just happened. Even if it's hard. That's why whenever someone leaves Basecamp, an immediate goodbye announcement is sent out companywide.

This announcement is written by either the person leaving or their manager. It's their choice (but most people who've left Basecamp chose to write their own). Either way, someone has to write one.

The person who's leaving then gets to see all the responses to this announcement from everyone else in the company before the day is up. These responses usually include sharing photos, memories, and stories. Saying goodbye is always hard, but it doesn't have to be formal or cold. We all know things change, circumstances shift, and shit happens.

Note: If their message to the company doesn't include exact details on why they are leaving, their manager will post a follow-up message the following week filling in the gaps. When someone leaves for another job, the whole story is usually shared by the person who's leaving. But when someone is let go, we often have to clarify once they're gone. It's important that the reasons are clear and no questions linger unanswered.

That's how you have calm goodbyes.

CHARLES DICKENS MAINTAINED A STRICT SCHEDULE COMPRISING FIVE HOURS OF WRITING IN SILENCE, FOLLOWED BY A THREE-HOUR WALK.

Dissect Your Process

The wrong time
for real-time

Following group chat at work is like being in an all-day meeting with random participants and no agenda. It's completely exhausting.

Chat puts conversations on conveyor belts that are perpetually moving away from you. If you're not at your station when the conversation rolls by, you'll never get a chance to put in your two cents. This means that if you want to have your say, you need be paying attention all day (and often to multiple rooms/channels). You can decide not to follow along, but then you're battling the fear of missing out. It's a bad bargain either way.

However, chat is not all bad if you use it sparingly. Chat is great for hashing stuff out quickly when speed truly is important. If there's a crisis or an emergency and you need to get a bunch of people aligned and on the same page quickly, chat's a good fit. (It's also great for watercooler-like social banter—goofing around, sharing silly pics—and generally building a camaraderie among people during gaps in the workday.)

But it's a mighty thin line when you're trapped in an ASAP chamber. All chat all the time conditions you to believe everything's worth discussing quickly right now, except that hardly anything is. Almost everything can and should wait until someone has had a chance to think it through and properly write it up.

Otherwise implied consensus is always lurking. "What do you mean you don't agree? We discussed it in the chat room." . . . "How was I supposed to know—I wasn't in there, I was working on something else." . . . "Oops, well, we discussed it and figured you were okay with it since you didn't chime in." . . . "WTF!" That's an all-too-common pattern when chat's where decisions get made.

When it comes to chat, we have two primary rules of thumb: "Real-time sometimes, asynchronous most of the time" and "If it's important, slow down."

Important topics need time, traction, and separation from the rest of the chatter. If something is being discussed in a chat room and it's clearly too important to process one line at a time, we ask people to "write it up" instead. This goes together with the rule "If everyone needs to see it, don't chat about it." Give the discussion a dedicated, permanent home that won't scroll away in five minutes.

There are lots of managers out there who love group chat because they can pop in and out quickly and speak to many people at once, but there are a lot of employees out there sweating all day long trying to keep up the appearance of being involved but knowing they have actual work to do.

It's common in the software industry to blame the users. It's the user's fault. They don't know how to use it. They're using it wrong. They need to do this or do that. But the reality is that specific designs encourage specific behaviors. If the design leads to stress, it's a bad design.

Chat is great as a small slice but not the whole pie of communication.

Dreadlines

Most deadlines aren't so much deadlines as *dreadlines*. Unrealistic dates mired by ever-expanding project requirements. More work piles on but the timeline remains the same. That's not work, that's hell.

Without a fixed, believable deadline, you can't work calmly. When you don't trust the date, or when you think it's impossible to do everything someone's telling you to do within a specific period of time, or when someone keeps piling on more work without giving you more time, you work frantically and maniacally. Few things are as demoralizing as working on projects with no end in sight.

That's not how we do it.

At Basecamp, we don't dread the deadline, we embrace it. Our deadlines remain fixed and fair. They are fundamental to our process—and making progress. If it's due on November 20, then it's due on November 20. The date won't move up and the date won't move back.

What's variable is the scope of the problem—the work itself. But only on the downside. You can't fix a deadline and then add more work to it. That's not fair. Our projects can only get smaller over time, not larger. As we progress, we separate the must-haves from the nice-to-haves and toss out the nonessentials.

And who makes the decision about what stays and what goes in a fixed period of time? The team that's working on it. Not the CEO, not the CTO. The team that's doing the work has control over the work. They wield the "scope hammer," as we call it. They can crush the big must-haves into smaller pieces and then judge each piece individually and objectively. Then they can sort, sift, and decide what's worth keeping and what can wait.

It's critical that the scope be flexible on the downside because almost everything that can take six months can also be done in some other form in six weeks. Likewise, small projects balloon into large projects all the time if you're not careful. It's all about knowing where to cut, when to say stop, and when to move on.

Another way to think about our deadlines is that they're based on budgets, not estimates. We're not fans of estimates because, let's face it, humans suck at estimating. But it turns out that people are quite good at setting and spending budgets. If we tell a team that they have six weeks to build *a great calendar feature* in Basecamp, they're much more likely to produce lovely work than if we ask them how long it'll take to build *this specific cal-*

endar feature, and then break their weekends and backs to make it so.

A deadline with a flexible scope invites pushback, compromises, and tradeoffs—all ingredients in healthy, calm projects. It's when you try to fix both scope and time that you have a recipe for dread, overwork, and exhaustion.

Here are some of the telltale signs that your deadline is really a dreadline:

- An unreasonably large amount of work that needs to be done in an unreasonably short amount of time. "This massive redesign and reorganization needs to happen in two weeks. Yeah, I know half the team is out on vacation next week, but that's not my problem."
- An unreasonable expectation of quality given the resources and time. "We can't compromise on quality—every detail must be perfect by Friday. Whatever it takes."
- An ever-expanding amount of work in the same time frame as originally promised. "The CEO just told me that we also need to launch this in Spanish and Italian, not just English."

Constraints are liberating, and realistic deadlines with flexible scopes can be just that. But they require you to embrace budgets and shun estimates. Great work will fill the time allotted if you allow it to.

Don't be a knee-jerk

At most companies, people put together a deck, reserve a conference room, and call a meeting to pitch a new idea. If they're lucky, no one interrupts them while they're presenting. (But usually someone jumps in and derails the presentation after two minutes.) When it's over, people *react*. This is precisely the problem.

The person making the pitch has presumably put a lot of time, thought, and energy into gathering their thoughts and presenting them clearly to an audience. But the rest of the people in the room are asked to react. Not absorb, not think it over, not consider—just react. Knee-jerk it. That's no way to treat fragile new ideas.

At Basecamp we flip the script.

When we present work, it's almost always written up first. A complete idea in the form of a carefully composed multipage document. Illustrated, whenever possible. And then it's posted to Basecamp, which lets everyone involved know there's a complete idea waiting to be considered.

139

Considered!

We don't want reactions. We don't want first impressions. We don't want knee-jerks. We want considered feedback. Read it over. Read it twice, three times even. Sleep on it. Take your time to gather and present your thoughts—just like the person who pitched the original idea took their time to gather and present theirs.

That's how you go deep on an idea.

Sometimes when people pitch ideas at Basecamp, there will be radio silence for a few days before a flood of feedback comes in. That's fine, and expected. Imagine a silent room after a physical meeting-style pitch. It would be awkward. And that's precisely why we prefer to present out-of-person, not in-person. We want silence and consideration to feel natural, not anxiety-provoking.

When we pitch this way, we're effectively "forcing the floor." No one can interrupt the presenter because there's no one there to interrupt. The idea is shared whole—there's no room to stop someone, no opportunity to break someone's flow. They have the floor and it can't be taken away. And then when you're ready to present your feedback, the floor is yours.

Give it a try sometime. Don't meet, write. Don't react, consider.

Watch out for 12-day weeks

Way back when, we used to release new software on Fridays all the time. That often meant working Saturdays and Sundays to fix an urgent problem with the new stuff, wrecking the weekend for whoever did the release. It was stupid yet predictable, because we kept setting deadlines at the end of a week. But Friday is the worst day to release anything.

First off, you probably rushed to finish. So work done on Fridays tends to be a bit sloppy.

Second, Mondays don't come after Fridays. Saturdays and Sundays come after Fridays. So if something goes wrong, you're working the weekend.

Third, if you work the weekends, you don't get a chance to recharge. Basically, when you've worked all week and you're forced to work the weekend, the following Monday is the eighth day of the last week, not the first day of next week. This means that if you keep working through that following week, you're working 12-day weeks. That's no good.

So here we were, creating unnecessary stress for ourselves. Stress that not only existed in the moment but that also lingered into the following week. Why?

We couldn't come up with a good reason, so instead of shipping big software updates on Fridays, we now wait until Monday the following week to do it. Yes, this introduced other risks—if we somehow make a big mistake, we're introducing it on the busiest day of the week. But knowing that also helps us be better prepared for the release. When there's more at stake, you tend to measure twice, cut once.

This encouraged us to take quality assurance more seriously, so we can catch more issues ahead of time. Reducing release-day stress was a multipronged approach. First comes recognition, then comes remediation.

Today shipping new software at Basecamp is almost entirely stress-free. There will always be some butterflies in the stomach—even a professional musician or public speaker gets nervous when they go onstage in front of a huge crowd. But stressed out we are not. And if we're feeling frenzied for any reason, we delay the release until we've calmed down.

THE POET AND CIVIL RIGHTS
ACTIVIST MAYA ANGELOU
PREFERRED TO WRITE ALONE
IN A MODEST HOTEL ROOM
AND WOULD WRAP UP AT 2 PM,
GIVING HERSELF ENOUGH TIME
TO DECOMPRESS BEFORE
DINNER WITH HER HUSBAND.

The new normal

Normal comes on quick.

First it starts as an outlier. Some behavior you don't love, but tolerate. Then someone else follows suit, but either you miss it or you let it slide. Then people pile on—repeating what they've seen because no one stepped in to course correct

Then it's too late. It's become the culture. The new normal.

This happens in organizations all the time. A single snarky remark can cascade into a storm of collective snark in the same way that a single spark can ignite a forest fire. And, implicitly, when you let it happen, it becomes okay. Behavior unchecked becomes behavior sanctioned.

We've gone down this path a number of times at Basecamp. There was a time when someone working a difficult case with a difficult customer could vent disparagingly in a company chat room, and nobody would say anything. Or we'd all rip on a company that made a mistake, forgetting that people in glass houses shouldn't throw stones.

We kinda knew it wasn't right, but we didn't stop it. Which just made it that much harder when we finally decided enough was enough.

Unwinding the new normal requires far more effort than preventing that new normal from being set in the first place. If you don't want gnarly roots in your culture, you have to mind the seeds.

You don't have to let something slide for long before it becomes the new normal. Culture is what culture does. Culture isn't what you intend it to be. It's not what you hope or aspire for it to be. It's what you do. So do better.

Bad habits beat
good intentions

Micromanagers tend to stay micromanagers.

Workaholics tend to stay workaholics.

Hustlers tend to stay hustlers.

What we do repeatedly hardens into habits. The longer you carry on, the tougher it is to change. All your best intentions about doing the right thing "later" are no match for the power of habits.

Yet people deceive themselves all the time. They think they can put in long hours for years "so I won't have to do it later." You may not *have* to do it, but you probably *will* do it. Because it's a habit.

Right from the beginning of Basecamp, we insisted on a reasonable workweek. We didn't pull all-nighters to make impossible deadlines. We scoped the work to fit a good day's work and then enjoyed a calm evening off. Not by magic, not by luck, but by choice.

If we had started by hiring a bunch of people we didn't need in the beginning, we would have continued to hire a bunch more people we don't need today. Instead, we hire when it hurts. Slowly, and only after we clearly need someone. Not in anticipation of possibly maybe.

If we had started by forcing everyone to come into the office to work, we'd almost certainly believe that the only way to work together would be to see each other face-to-face every day. Instead, today we have people working full-time for us in dozens of cities around the world. They work at their own pace, in their own place.

When calm starts early, calm becomes the habit. But if you start crazy, it'll define you. You have to keep asking yourself if the way you're working today is the way you'd want to work in 10, 20, or 30 years. If not, now is the time to make a change, not "later."

Later is where excuses live. Later is where good intentions go to die. Later is a broken back and a bent spirit. Later says "all-nighters are temporary until we've got this figured out." Unlikely. Make the change now.

Independencies

Few question the assumption that a company should always strive to move in sync. Team A providing Team B with exactly what they need exactly when they need it. All lined up, beautifully choreographed. But such a ballet of interdependence is a performance we'd rather skip.

We want our teams to be able to glide by one another independently rather than get tripped up in lockstep. Things should fit together rather than stick together.

Dependencies are tangled, intertwined teams, groups, or individuals that can't move independently of one another. Whenever someone is waiting on someone else, there's a dependency in the way.

If you're building airplanes or working an assembly line, fine. That's probably required. But most companies these days aren't, yet they still work as if they are.

We've fallen into the dependency trap a few times. For example, we used to try to line up release schedules for our web app and mobile apps. If we had something new on the web app, it had to wait until the iPhone and Android versions also had it before we could release everything. That slowed us down, tangled us up, and led to self-imposed frustrations. In the end, Android users didn't care whether they were using exactly the same design as iPhone users.

We also frequently used to bundle five or six major new features together in one big-bang release rather than shipping each new improvement when ready. It makes for a great splash, but big-bang releases bundle the risk from every component, so if one thing falls behind, the whole thing can get held up. Which it always does. So you end up with a much higher risk of significantly delayed delivery or, at worst, having to scrap everything.

Throwing away a bunch of work, simply because of the way you worked on it, is a morale gut punch. But that's what happens when your work is filled with dependencies.

Today we ship things when they're ready rather than when they're coordinated. If it's ready for the web, ship it! iOS will catch up when they're ready. Or if iOS is first, Android will get there when they're ready. The same is true for the web. Customers get the value when it's ready wherever, not when it's ready everywhere.

So don't tie more knots, cut more ties. The fewer bonds, the better.

Commitment, not consensus

The gold standard for legal deliberations is a unanimous verdict by a jury of peers. When the stakes of justice are at their highest, consensus is the only thing that'll do. Anything less and it's a do-over.

That's a wonderful ideal for a criminal court, but it's a terrible practice to mimic in business. If you only have to make a single decision, and it might literally be life or death, then that's a burden worth bearing. But in business, you may have to make multiple major decisions monthly. If every one of them has to be made by consensus, you're in for an endless grind with significant collateral damage. The cost of consensus is simply too much to pay over and over again.

When you get a bunch of people in a room under the assumption that consensus is the only way out again, you're in for a war of attrition. Whoever can keep arguing the longest stands the best chance of winning. That's just silly.

So what to do instead? It's not like good decisions just spring into the mind of a single individual. They're always going to be the product of consultation, evidence, arguments, and debate. But the only sustainable method in business is to have them *made* by individuals.

Someone in charge has to make the final call, even if others would prefer a different decision. Good decisions don't so much need consensus as they need commitment.

Jeff Bezos put it well in his 2017 letter to shareholders:

> I disagree and commit all the time. We recently green-lit a particular Amazon Studios original. I told the team my view: debatable whether it would be interesting enough, complicated to produce, the business terms aren't that good, and we have lots of other opportunities. They had a completely different opinion and wanted to go ahead. I wrote back right away with "I disagree and commit and hope it becomes the most watched thing we've ever made." Consider how much slower this decision cycle would have been if the team had actually had to *convince* me rather than simply get my commitment.

We totally agree. We've been practicing disagree and commit since the beginning, but it took Bezos's letter to name the practice. Now we even use that exact term in our discussions. "I disagree, but let's commit" is something you'll hear at Basecamp after heated debates about specific products or strategy decisions.

Companies waste an enormous amount of time and energy trying to convince everyone to agree before moving forward on something. What they'll often get is reluctant acceptance that masks secret resentment.

Instead, they should allow everyone to be heard and then turn the decision over to one person to make the final call. It's their job to listen, consider, contemplate, and decide.

Calm companies get this. Everyone's invited to pitch their ideas, make their case, and have their say, but then the decision is left to someone else. As long as people are truly heard and it's repeatedly demonstrated that their voice matters, those who shared will understand that even if things don't fall their way this time.

Last thing: What's especially important in disagree-and-commit situations is that the final decision should be explained clearly to everyone involved. It's not just decide and go, it's decide, explain, and go.

Compromise on quality

We compromise on quality all the time at Basecamp. We launch features that aren't good enough for everyone (but will be Just Fine for plenty of people). We duct-tape bugs when they're not bad enough to warrant a true root-cause fix. We publish essays on our blog that may have a grammatical error or two.

You just can't bring your A game to every situation. Knowing when to embrace Good Enough is what gives you the opportunity to be truly excellent when you need to be.

We're not suggesting you put shit work out there. You need to be able to be proud of it, even if it's only "okay." But attempting to be indiscriminately great at everything is a foolish waste of energy.

Rather than put endless effort into every detail, we put lots of effort into separating what really matters from what sort of matters from what doesn't matter at all. The act of separation should be your highest-quality endeavor. It's easy to say "Everything has to be great," but anyone can do that. The challenge lies in figuring out where you can be just kinda okay or even downright weak.

Think of it this way. If you do one thing at 100 percent, you've spent 100 percent to get that one thing. If you spend 20 percent each on getting five things to 80 percent, well, then, you've done five things! We'll almost always take that trade.

Being clear about what demands excellence and what's perfectly okay just being adequate is a great way to bring a sense of calm into your work. You'll worry less, you'll accept more. "That's fine" is such a wonderfully relaxing way to work most of the time. Save the occasional scrutiny for the differentiating details that truly matter.

Narrow as you go

It's almost impossible to work on something and not be tempted to chase all the exciting new what-if and we-could-also ideas that come up. There's always one more thing it could do, one more improvement it should have. But if you actually want to make progress, you have to narrow as you go.

After the initial dust settles, the work required to finish a project should be dwindling over time, not expanding. The deadline should be comfortably approaching, not scarily arriving. Remember: Deadlines, not dreadlines.

When we spend six weeks on something, the first week or two is for clarifying unknowns and validating assumptions. This is the time when the concept needs to hit reality and either bounce if it's sound or shatter if it's not.

That's why we quickly begin prototyping as soon as we can in those first two weeks. We're often looking at something real within a day or two. Nothing tells the truth like actually experiencing the idea in real life. That's the first time we know if what we had in our heads is actually going to work or not.

But after that—after that brief period of exploration at the beginning of a project—it's time to focus in and get narrow. It's time for tunnel vision!

This runs against the church of endless exploration. That constant chase for the better idea. If we just brainstormed a little more . . . riffed a little more . . . explored a little more . . . pulled in a few more people to collaborate with . . . Nope.

Once the initial exploration is over, every week should lead us closer to being done, not further from it. Commit to an idea. See it through. Make it happen. You can always go back later, but only if you actually finish.

Week four of a six-week project should be about finishing things up and ramping things down, not coming up with big new ideas.

It's not that new approaches or ideas are bad, but their timing may well be. Always keeping the door open to radical changes only invites chaos and second-guessing. Confidently close that door. Accept that better ideas aren't necessarily better if they arrive after the train has left the station. If they're so good, they can catch the next one.

That's really the answer to new ideas that arrive too late: You'll just have to wait!

Why not nothing?

"Doing nothing isn't an option."

Oh, yes, it is. And it's often the best one.

"Nothing" should always be on the table.

Change makes things worse all the time. It's easier to fuck up something that's working well than it is to genuinely improve it. But we commonly delude ourselves into thinking that more time, more investment, more attention is always going to win.

Case in point: We were working on revamping the way clients and firms work together using Basecamp. We were planning on replacing the old way with the new way. That meant, at some point, moving everyone who used the old way over to the new way. That meant migrating data, converting formats, and shoving an entirely different experience in their faces.

But what if someone liked the old way? Or not even liked it, but simply was comfortable with it? Sometimes we assume that someone has to like or dislike something. Often they just get used to something and that's what they prefer. Taking that away is a violent act, not a gentle one.

So halfway through the project we paused. What if we did nothing? No forced change, no migration, no new experience for those who preferred the old way? What if existing customers could use what they already had and we only gave the new way to new customers who never knew the old way?

So that's what we did. Nothing. No forced migration, no requirement to learn something new, no hard sell on how "this is actually better." Things would stay exactly as they were for current customers (but they could also opt into the new approach if they wanted to).

Nothing was better for customers. And, self-servingly, nothing was better for us, too. It meant less work, it meant shrinking the project, it meant shaving weeks off the deadline, and it meant shipping sooner. Nothing was better.

Sometimes you have to fight against the obvious. And sometimes you have to recognize that time in doesn't equal benefits out. Doing nothing can be the hardest choice but the strongest, too.

It's enough

Calm requires getting comfortable with enough.

While there's no hard-line definition of when's enough or what's enough in every situation, one thing's for sure: If it's *never* enough, then it'll always be crazy at work.

A few years ago, we looked at the time it took to answer emails from customers. Sometimes it took hours. While that might seem fast to a lot of people accustomed to waiting days for a reply, it wasn't fast enough for us.

So we started by setting a target: one hour. The vast majority of the hundreds of customers writing to us every day should get a response within one hour. No autoresponders, just real humans. Real fast.

To do that, we hired up, plastered the fast response promise on our website, started responding quicker and quicker, and began beaming with pride at our newfound capability.

Then we got greedy for more. Hey, if we can get down to one hour, why not 30 minutes? So we did that. Why not 15 minutes? So we did that. WHY NOT TWO MINUTES? SO. WE. DID. THAT!

Seriously, two minutes. Some in even one minute!

And why not, right? Why not be as fast as possible? You can never get back to people fast enough, right?

Wrong.

Answering hundreds of emails every day within a minute or two just isn't sustainable. The team that had beamed with pride over hitting those numbers started getting stressed out. Some began to feel bad if it took three minutes to get back to someone when our average response time was only two minutes.

Imagine that—feeling *bad* about getting back to a customer within three minutes! We had stumbled into an unrealistic goal of "we can never get back to people fast enough" and it was taking its toll. It was amazing that it could be done, but we had forgotten to ask whether it *should* be done.

So we pulled back.

No doubt, customers loved hearing back from us quickly. Many of them told us so. They were amazed, really. But, as we found, they were equally amazed at 5 minutes, 10 minutes, or even within the hour. Their expectations were that they'd either never hear back or it would take maybe a day or so. So to hear back in, say, 15 minutes just blew them away all the same.

We just needed to be fast enough and 15 minutes was fast enough. Even within the hour was fast enough.

That popped the pressure release valve on our team, too. Everyone calmed down. They could spend more time thinking, helping, and writing—and less time rushing. Everything got better. Customers remained thrilled with our fast service—which was a bit slower than before but still way ahead of the industry—and our team chilled out and did better work. Win-win.

Not only was it enough, it was plenty.

Worst practices

Every mature industry is drowning in best practices. There are best practices about how to price a product, conduct employee reviews, do content marketing, design a website, or make an app scalable to millions of users. There's no end to advice claiming to be the best.

Yet so much of it is not merely bullshit but quite possibly the worst thing you could do. What counts as the best practice for a company of 10,000 is very rarely so for a company of 10.

Hell, even our own internal best practices at Basecamp that were set when we only had 7 people at the company failed or held us back when we grew to 30. We've frequently been trapped by things that used to work well but no longer do.

And it's not just about a difference in size, it's a difference in everything. Are you selling a service for a recurring fee or a product for a onetime cost? Different practices. Are you just designing for a single awesome iPhone app or are you trying to reach Android, the web, and email as well? Different practices. Are you building your company to last, or are you starting with an exit strategy in mind? Different practices. Have your people worked together for a long time, or are you building a brand-new team from scratch? Different practices.

There are many reasons to be skeptical of best practices, but one of the most common is when you see someone deriving them purely from outside observations about how another company does it: "Top 10 best practices for how Apple develops products." Has that person worked on a product development team at Apple? No. They're simply coming to their own conclusions based on their own assumptions about how they think things work. Unless you've actually done the work, you're in no position to encode it as a best practice.

Furthermore, many best practices are purely folklore. No one knows where they came from, why they started, and why they continue to be followed. But because of that powerful label—best practice—people often forget to even question them. Someone much smarter than us must have come up with them, right? Everyone who follows them is experiencing great success, right? If we aren't doing well by them, it's got to be our fault, right? Most of those rights are probably wrongs.

What's more, best practices imply that there's a single answer to whatever question you're facing. It implies that you really don't have a choice in the matter. Resist the implication. You always have a choice.

All this isn't to say that best practices are of no value. They're like training wheels. When you don't know how to keep your balance or how fast to pedal, they can be helpful to get you going. But every best practice should come with a reminder to reconsider.

And, ultimately, you can't develop a calm culture if you're constantly fretting about what the best practices prescribe and whether you're measuring or messing up. Find what works for you and do that. Create your practices and your patterns. Who cares if they're the best for anyone else.

NOVELIST HARUKI MURAKAMI WRITES INTERNATIONAL BEST-SELLERS AND GETS TO BED BY 9PM EVERY NIGHT.

Whatever it doesn't take

"Whatever it takes!" It feels good, doesn't it? It's hard to find three words loaded with more inspiration, aspiration, and ambition than "whatever it takes!" It's the rallying cry for captains of industry and war generals alike. Who wouldn't want to be such a hero and a leader?

But you're not actually capturing a hill on the beach of Normandy, are you? You're probably just trying to meet some arbitrary deadline set by those who don't actually have to do the work. Or trying to meet some fantastical financial "stretch goal" that nobody who actually has to do the stretching would think reasonable.

Whatever it takes is an iceberg. Steer clear lest it literally sink your ship. Just ask Edward Smith, the captain of the *Titanic*, who gave orders to do whatever it took to get to New York faster than expected to break a record. You probably know how that turned out.

Reasonable expectations are out the window with whatever it takes. So you know you're going to grossly underestimate the difficulty and complexity required to make it happen.

You almost surely haven't budgeted time, energy, or dollars for whatever it takes. That's code for "at all costs." When you stop discussing costs, you know they're going to spiral.

You probably aren't ready to say no to all the things you'll have to skip out on because you said yes to whatever it takes.

Whatever it takes means you'll probably be working at 10 p.m. on Wednesday. And Thursday. And Friday.

Whatever it takes means sloppy work in the service of just delivering something.

Whatever it takes means if you won't do it, your boss will find someone else who will (endure the abuse).

If you're in business long enough, there certainly will be rare moments when whatever it takes is truly called for. A real, honest emergency. Or maybe because you won't be able to make payroll. Or maybe because inaction will permanently scar your reputation. So yes, there are moments. Rare, extreme moments. Don't drive your everyday business by the fear of those outliers.

Here's what we do. Rather than demand whatever it takes, we ask, What *will* it take? That's an invitation to a conversation. One where we can discuss strategy, make tradeoffs, make cuts, come up with a simpler approach all together, or even decide it's not worth it after all. Questions bring options, decrees burn them.

Have less to do

Time-management hacks, life hacks, sleep hacks, work hacks. These all reflect an obsession with trying to squeeze more time out of the day, but rearranging your daily patterns to find more time for work isn't the problem. Too much shit to do is the problem.

The only way to get more done is to have less to do.

Saying no is the only way to claw back time. Don't shuffle 12 things so that you can do them in a different order, don't set timers to move on from this or that. Eliminate 7 of the 12 things, and you'll have time left for the 5. It's not time management, it's obligation elimination. Everything else is snake oil.

Besides, time isn't something that can be managed. Time is time—it rolls along at the same pace regardless of how you try to wrestle with it. What you choose to spend it on is the only thing you have control over.

Management scholar Peter Drucker nailed it decades ago when he said "There is nothing so useless as doing efficiently that which should not be done at all." Bam!

At Basecamp we've become ruthless about eliminating either work that doesn't need to be done or work we don't want to do.

For example, we used to accept payment by credit card and check. Credit cards were entirely automated, so on our side it didn't take anyone's time to process. But checks were mailed in. Which meant someone needed to receive them, process them, deal with incorrect amounts, tie them correctly to the account they were associated with, etc.

Now, some companies might say, "Hey, okay, let's hire someone else who can do that specific work." Others might say, "Let's spend some time, money, and technology to automate the process some more."

What did we say? "We won't accept checks anymore." Yes, we decided to turn away revenue and customers who could only pay by check. But it wasn't really a turn away, it was a trade away. We traded some revenue for some time.

We didn't encourage someone to carve out time in their day to deal with manual check processing. Instead, we eliminated work that had to be done by saying no—no more checks.

There are surely dozens more things we don't need to be doing at work. We're forever on the lookout, and always on the hunt to track them down. Not so that we can check them off the list, but so we can throw them away.

Three's company

Nearly all product work at Basecamp is done by teams of three people. It's our magic number. A team of three is usually composed of two programmers and one designer. And if it's not three, it's one or two rather than four or five. We don't throw more people at problems, we chop problems down until they can be carried across the finish line by teams of three.

We rarely have meetings at Basecamp, but when we do, you'll hardly ever find more than three people around a table. Same with conference calls or video chats. Any conversation with more than three people is typically a conversation with too many people.

What if there are five departments involved in a project or a decision? There aren't. We don't work on projects like that— intentionally.

What is it with three? Three is a wedge, and that's why it works. Three has a sharp point. It's an odd number, so there are no ties. It's powerful enough to make a dent, but also weak enough to not break what isn't broken. Big teams make things worse all the time by applying too much force to things that only need to be lightly finessed.

The problem with four is that you almost always need to add a fifth to manage. The problem with five is that it's two too many. And six, seven, or eight on a team will inevitably make simple things more complicated than they need to be. Just like work expands to fill the time available, work expands to fill the *team* available. Small, short projects quickly become big, long projects when too many people are there to work on them.

You can do big things with small teams, but it's a whole hell of a lot harder to do small things with big teams. And small things are often all that's necessary. The occasional big thing is great, but most improvements come as small incremental steps. Big teams can step right over those small moves.

Three keeps you honest. It tempers your ambition in all the right ways. It requires you to make tradeoffs. And most important, three reduces miscommunication and improves coordination. Three people can talk directly with one another without introducing hearsay. And it's a lot easier to coordinate three people's schedules than four or more.

We love three.

Stick with it

If the boss is constantly pulling people off one project to chase another, nobody's going to get anything done.

"Pull-offs" can happen for a number of reasons, but the most common one is that someone senior has a new idea that Just Can't Wait.

These half-baked, right-in-the-middle-of-something-else new ideas lead to half-finished, abandoned projects that litter the landscape and zap morale.

That's why rather than jumping on every new idea right away, we make every idea wait a while. Generally a few weeks, at least. That's just enough time either to forget about it completely or to realize you can't stop thinking about it.

What makes this pause possible is that our projects don't go on forever. Six weeks max, and generally shorter. That means we have natural opportunities to consider new ideas every few weeks. We don't have to cut something short to start something new. First we finish what we started, then we consider what we want to tackle next. When the urgency of now goes away, so does the anxiety.

This approach also prevents unfinished work from piling up. Having a box full of stale work is no fun. Happiness is shipping: finishing good work, sending it off, and then moving on to the next idea.

Besides, the next morning (or week) has a way of telling the truth. It's good to sleep on something. You might well wake up the next day to see what was the world's best idea yesterday doesn't seem quite as important now. Taking a breather gives you perspective.

So give it five minutes, keep your energy focused on finishing what you're working on now, and then decide what to do next once you're done and ready to take on new work.

Know no

No is easier to do, yes is easier to say.

No is no to one thing.

Yes is no to a thousand things.

No is a precision instrument, a surgeon's scalpel, a laser beam focused on one point.

Yes is a blunt object, a club, a fisherman's net that catches everything indiscriminately.

No is specific.

Yes is general.

When you say no to one thing, it's a choice that breeds choices. Tomorrow you can be as open to new opportunities as you were today.

When you say yes to one thing, you've spent that choice. The door is shut on a whole host of alternative possibilities and tomorrow is that much more limited.

When you say no now, you can come back and say yes later.

If you say yes now, it's harder to say no later.

No is calm but hard.

Yes is easy but a flurry.

Knowing what you'll say no to is better than knowing what you'll say yes to.

Know no.

COMPOSER GUSTAV MAHLER
WROTE HIS SYMPHONIES
DURING SOLITARY SUMMERS
IN THE ALPS, WHERE HE
WORKED IN A SMALL COTTAGE
AND WALKED FOR HOURS
AFTER WORK.

Mind Your Business

Risk without putting yourself at risk

A lot of entrepreneurs are addicted to risk. The bigger the better. Chasing the thrill, the adrenaline, and the glory that comes from hanging in the balance between winning everything or losing it all. Not us.

We don't need to shoot up on risk to get excited about work. We'll take a risk, but we won't put the company at risk.

For example, we recently did something that would appear incredibly risky: We more than tripled the entry price of Basecamp. We went from $29/month to $99/month.

We made some significant improvements to the product at the same time. And the new price didn't apply to everyone—existing Basecamp customers were grandfathered in at their current prices. But new customers signing up for Basecamp after we made the change were charged $99/month.

Did we test it? No. Did we ask people if they'd be willing to pay more? No. Were we sure it would work? Absolutely not. Sounds risky!

But really, what was the risk? Would we go out of business if it didn't work? No. Would we have to lay people off if this wild experiment fell flat? No. Why not? Because we already had a massive base of more than 100,000 customers paying us what they were before.

We promised ourselves to give it six months and see how it turned out. We'd tweak it along the way. A big step first and then small steps as we went. And we could always walk it back if it flopped. That's managed, calculated risk with a safety rope attached.

As it turned out, tripling the entry price worked out great. We gave up some new signups, but we more than made up for it with the higher price. That's what we were aiming for. Bull's-eye!

Taking a risk doesn't have to be reckless. You're not any bolder or braver because you put yourself or the business at needless risk. The smart bet is one where you get to play again if it doesn't come up your way.

Season's greetings

Change is often seen as stressful, but the polar opposite, monotony, can be even worse. You can only work exactly the same way, at the same pace, doing the same work for so long before monotony bites.

When you're growing up, life is seasonal. Even if you live in a place where the weather doesn't change, there's a change in rhythm to the year. There's school, there's summer. Different things happen at different times.

But unless you work in a seasonal business, work in March is usually the same as work in May. June's the same as January. And it would be hard to tell December's work from February's work. Not at Basecamp.

We celebrate the summer months (in the Northern Hemisphere, at least) by cutting out a workday every week. May through September we work 4-day, 32-hour weeks. The idea isn't to cram more stuff into fewer hours, so we adapt our ambition, too. Winter is when we buckle down and take on larger, more challenging projects. Summer, with its shorter 4-day weeks, is when we tackle simpler, lighter projects.

We also celebrate the seasons outside of work at Basecamp by covering the cost of a weekly community-supported agriculture share for each employee. Fresh, local, seasonal fruits and veggies in people's homes. This is a year-round benefit, but the bounty naturally changes with the seasons. It's a delicious, healthy way to celebrate change.

Be it in hours, degrees of difficulty, or even specific benefits that emphasize seasonality, find ways to melt the monotony of work. People grow dull and stiff if they stay in the same swing for too long.

Calm's in the black

From the very first month we started the business back in 1999, we were profitable. We've remained profitable every year since then.

We've certainly had our share of good fortune and luck, but we've also intentionally never gotten ahead of ourselves. We've always kept our costs in check and never made a move that would push us back from black to red.

Why? Because crazy's in the red. Calm's in the black.

Until you're running a profitable business, you're always almost out of business. You're racing the runway. Fretting about whether you'll take off in time. Worrying about how to make payroll at the last moment if you don't. Talk about a pressurized environment!

When companies are in the red, employees worry about their jobs. People aren't stupid—they know that burning cash means the good times won't last. The possibility of layoffs is always nagging. CVs are always at the ready.

Revenue alone is no defense, either, because revenue without a profit margin isn't going to save you. You can easily go broke generating revenue—many companies have. But you can't go broke generating a profit.

Profit means time to think, space to explore. It means being in control of your own destiny and schedule.

Without profit, something is always on fire. When companies talk about burn rates, two things are burning: money and people. One you're burning up, one you're burning out.

ASTROPHYSICIST SANDRA FABER,
WHO HAS MADE GROUNDBREAKING
DISCOVERIES ABOUT DARK
MATTER AND HOW GALAXIES ARE
FORMED, SAID HER WORK
BENEFITED FROM A DAILY
ROUTINE WHERE SHE'D FOCUS ON
HER FAMILY DURING EVENINGS
AND WEEKENDS.

Priced to lose

The worst customer is the one you can't afford to lose. The big whale that can crush your spirit and fray your nerves with just a hint of their dissatisfaction. These are the customers who keep you up at night.

Yet most business-software companies, like ours, are irresistibly drawn to the siren song of huge accounts. That's because most business software is sold by the seat.

For example, sell to a small company with 7 people at $10/user and you'll get a customer worth $70/month. But land a company with 120 employees at $10/user and you score a contract worth $1,200/month. Then think what a 1,200-employee account would do. Or a 12,000-employee account.

You can see why huge company accounts are so attractive—and addicting.

We've rejected the per-seat business model from day one. It's not because we don't like money, but because we like our freedom more!

The problem with per-seat pricing is that it makes your biggest customers your best customers. With money comes influence, if not outright power. And from that flows decisions about what and who to spend time on. There's no way to be immune from such pressure once the money is flowing. The only fix is to cap the spigot.

So we take the opposite approach. Buy Basecamp today and it's just $99/month, flat and fixed. It doesn't matter if you have 5 employees, 50, 500, or 5,000—it's still just $99/month total. You can't pay us more than that.

On the face of it, such a model makes no sense. Any first-year MBA student will tell you as much. You're leaving money on the table! You're letting your biggest customers get too much of a bargain! They wouldn't bat an eye paying 10 times or even 100 times as much!

Thanks but no thanks. Here are a couple of reasons why:

First, since no one customer can pay us an outsized amount, no one customer's demands for features or fixes or exceptions will automatically rise to the top. This leaves us free to make software for ourselves and on behalf of a broad base of customers, not at the behest of any single one or a privileged few. It's a lot easier to do the right thing for the many when you don't fear displeasing a few super customers.

Second, we wanted to build Basecamp for small businesses like ourselves: members of the Fortune 5,000,000. And not just build software for them, but really help them. To be honest, we don't really give a shit about the Fortune 500. The corporate behemoths are much more likely to be set in stone, unable to change. With the Fortune 5,000,000 we have a real shot at making a real impact. That's more satisfying work.

Third, we didn't want to get sucked into the mechanics that chasing big contracts inevitably leads to. Key account managers. Sales meetings. Schmoozing. The enterprise sales playbook is well established and repulsive to us. But it's also unavoidable once you open the door to the big bucks from the big shots. Again, no thank you.

But then why not just do both? Sell to small businesses on one model and also have a group of people dedicated to servicing big businesses? Because we don't want to be a two-headed company with two cultures. Selling to small businesses and selling to enterprises take two very different approaches with two very different kinds of people.

Becoming a calm company is all about making decisions about who you are, who you want to serve, and who you want to say no to. It's about knowing what to optimize for. It's not that any particular choice is the right one, but not making one or dithering is definitely the wrong one.

Launch and learn

If you want to know the truth about what you've built, you have to ship it. You can test, you can brainstorm, you can argue, you can survey, but only shipping will tell you whether you're going to sink or swim.

Is this thing any good? Does it solve a real problem? Should we have made it better? Are we making what customers want? Is anybody going to buy this? Did we price it right?

All good questions!

But you can debate this internally forever. And many companies do. In the search for answers, they find anxiety instead. Second guesses, fear, and indecision fill the hallways in offices around the world.

But why worry? Do your best, believe in the work you've done, and ship it. Then you'll find out for sure.

Maybe it'll be spot-on. Maybe it'll suck. Maybe it'll be somewhere in between. But if you want to know, you have to put it on the market. The real market. It's the only place you'll find the truth.

You can follow the spec. You can test it forever. You can talk to potential customers and ask them what they'd pay for this thing you're making. You can run surveys and ask people if they'd buy your product if it did this thing or that thing.

But so what? Those are simulated answers, they aren't real.

Real answers are only uncovered when someone's motivated enough to buy your product and use it in their own natural environment—and of their own volition. Anything else is a simulation, and simulated situations give you simulated answers. Shipping real products gives you real answers.

At Basecamp we live this philosophy to the extreme. We don't show any customers anything until every customer can see it. We don't beta-test with customers. We don't ask people what they'd pay for something. We don't ask anyone what they think of something. We do the best job we know how to do and then we launch it into the market. The market will tell us the truth.

Do we miss things we could have found had we asked a bunch of people beforehand? Of course. But at what cost? Putting everything we build in front of customers beforehand is slow, costly, and results in a mountain of prerelease feedback that has to be sifted through, considered, debated, discussed, and decided upon. And yet it's still all just a guess! That's a lot of energy to spend guessing.

So do your best and put it out there. You can iterate from there on real insights and real answers from real customers who really do need your product. Launch and learn.

Promise not to promise

Since the beginning of Basecamp, we've been loath to make promises about future product improvements. We've always wanted customers to judge the product they could buy and use today, not some imaginary version that might exist in the future.

It's why we've never committed to a product road map. It's not because we have a secret one in the back of some smoky room we don't want to share, but because one doesn't actually exist. We honestly don't know what we'll be working on in a year, so why act like we do?

But when we recently launched an all-new version of Basecamp, we ended up making a promise about the future anyway. D'oh.

See, the new version didn't initially include a feature our customers were clamoring for: project templates. The requests piled in, the emails piled up. We wanted to do it, but we weren't sure when we'd be able to get to it. So we just told people "by the end of the year." At the time that gave us eight months or so—which sounded easy—but it discounted all the work it would take to get it done as well as all the other stuff we also had to do at the same time.

March ticked by. Then April. Then May, June, July, and August. We still hadn't started on the project templates feature. And then September, and October comes along, and now, to come through on our promise, we had to drop a bunch of other things we wanted to do so that we could deliver project templates before the year ended. It was a great feature, and customers ultimately loved it, but we had to rush it. That's what promises lead to—rushing, dropping, scrambling, and a tinge of regret at the earlier promise that was a bit too easy to make.

Promises pile up like debt, and they accrue interest, too. The longer you wait to fulfill them, the more they cost to pay off and the worse the regret. When it's time to do the work, you realize just how expensive that yes really was.

Many companies are weighed down by all sorts of prior obligations to placate. Promises salespeople made to land a deal. Promises the project manager made to the client. Promises the owner made to the employees. Promises one department made to another.

Saying "Yes, later" is the easy way out of anything. You can only extend so many promises before you've spent all your future energy. Promises are easy and cheap to make, actual work is hard and expensive. If it wasn't, you'd just have done it now rather than promised it later.

FRENCH INTELLECTUAL AND
WRITER SIMONE DE BEAUVOIR
BROKE UP HER DAY BY TAKING
A FOUR-HOUR BREAK EACH
AFTERNOON TO VISIT FRIENDS.

Copycats

And if the whole world's singing your songs
And all of your paintings have been hung
Just remember what was yours
Is everyone's from now on
And that's not wrong or right
But you can struggle with it all you like
You'll only get uptight

—Wilco, "What Light"

You can get red-faced and furious that a competitor copied your product, stole your design, and reapportioned your ideas. But what good does it do?

Getting angry only hurts you. It zaps energy you could have spent doing better work still. It blurs your focus on what's next, keeping you locked in on the past. And again, for what?

Do you think that competitor is going to have a revelation and realize the error in their ways because you got upset? If they had such insight, they probably wouldn't have copied you in the first place.

Do you think your customers are going to care? They just want a good product at a great price. Few will have the time or empathy for a sob story about what the competition did or didn't do.

We've been ripped off and cloned a hundred times (and that's probably underestimating it). Our designs have been lifted wholesale from our product. Our words repurposed and used against us. Our ideas hijacked and attributed elsewhere.

That's life! If you want to be calm, you have to move on.

To be fair, it used to bother us. In the early days, when everything was so fragile it was easy to freak when you saw your stuff with someone else's name on it. What's worse is when it's a poor copy! Then you're just pissed that someone else is making you look bad.

But, really, unless you've patented it, there's not a whole lot you can do about it. Besides, copying does more harm to the copier than to the copied. When someone copies you, they are copying a moment in time. They don't know the thinking that went into getting you to that moment in time, and they won't know the thinking that'll help you have a million more moments in time. They're stuck with what you left behind.

So, really, chill out. Accept the mild frustration for a moment and then let it go.

Change control

You'll often hear that people don't like change, but that's not quite right. People have no problem with change they asked for. What people don't like is forced change—change they didn't request on a timeline they didn't choose. Your "new and improved" can easily become their "what the fuck?" when it is dumped on them as a surprise.

We've learned that lesson over and over again making Basecamp. We'd come up with a new design that moved the stuff around a bit too much to make room for something better, and all we'd hear is "WHAT DID YOU DO TO MY APP! I LIKED IT JUST HOW IT WAS! CHANGE IT BACK!"

The standard playbook in software is to dismiss users like that. Hey, this is the price of progress, and progress is always good, always better. That's myopic and condescending. For many customers, better doesn't matter when comfort, consistency, and familiarity are higher up on their value chain.

This doesn't mean your new work sucks, just that people are usually in the middle of something that's more important *to them* than a change *to your* product. They're already invested in what they have to do and they're already familiar with how they're going to do it. And then you toss a change at them that immediately makes their life a little more complicated. Now they have a new thing to learn right in the middle of having an old thing to do.

It's taken us a long time and a number of missteps to learn this core truth about selling: Sell new customers on the new thing and let old customers keep whatever they already have. This is the way to keep the peace and maintain the calm.

This is why we still run three completely different versions of Basecamp: our original software that we sold from 2004 to 2012, our second version that we sold from 2012 to 2015, and our third version that launched in 2015. Every new version was "better," but we never force anyone to upgrade to a new version. If you signed up for the original version back in 2007, you can keep using that forever. And a significant number still do (and we love that)!

So why didn't we just stop and stick with the original version of Basecamp? Because we've had new ideas along the way. Technology and design has changed. We've evolved. But our evolution is at our pace, and new customers today expect something different than new customers did a decade ago. But that doesn't mean we should force our earliest customers to follow along at our pace.

It also doesn't mean you shouldn't invite your customers to check out your latest offering. But it should be an invitation, not a demand. Once you start pushing too hard, some will rightfully resist and then suddenly you're in a skirmish. There's nothing calm about that.

It's not free to honor old agreements or maintain old products. That's the price of having a legacy. That's the price of being successful enough that you have customers who liked you before you made your most recent thing. You should celebrate that! Be proud of your heritage.

Startups are easy, stayups are hard

Many entrepreneurs put everything they have into starting their business. Long nights, loads of focus, and lots of love. And then they launch, utterly exhausted by the sprint. Now it's finally done, they think. If only!

Getting things off the ground is so hard that it's natural to expect it'll just get easier from here. Except it doesn't. Things get harder as you go, not easier. The easiest day is day one. That's the dirty little secret of business.

As you grow, you hire people. With people come personalities. With personalities come office politics and a hundred other challenges of human nature.

As customers start to notice you, so does the competition. Now you're in someone else's crosshairs. When you were launching, you were all offense. Now you have to worry about playing defense, too.

Before you know it, your costs balloon. It becomes more expensive to keep the lights on. Profits seem further away as you grow and expand.

Sound like gloom and doom? It's not! Not at all—it's all really exciting. But it's also reality. Business gets harder after you launch.

So it makes sense to mentally prepare for what comes after launch. If you think it's all sunshine and roses ahead, you're going to be caught off guard. If you understand what the future might look like, you can visualize it and be ready when the rain doesn't let up. It's all about setting expectations.

Ultimately, startups are easy, stayups are hard. Keeping the show running for the long term is a lot harder than walking onstage for the first time. On day one, every startup in the world is in business. On day one thousand, only a fraction remain standing. That's reality. So pace yourself. Don't burn out early thinking the hard part is behind you.

PLAYWRIGHT TONY KUSHNER
WRITES LONGHAND WITH FOUNTAIN
PENS ON YELLOW LEGAL PADS,
AND STOPS WHEN HE RUNS
OUT OF INK.

No big deal or the end of the world?

Here's something that should be obvious: People don't like to have their grievances downplayed or dismissed. When that happens, even the smallest irritation can turn into an obsessive crusade.

Imagine you're staying at a hotel, and the air-conditioning isn't working right. You call the front desk to mention it, and they say, oh yeah, they know about that, and someone is going to come fix that next week (after you've left). In the meantime, could you just open a window (down to that noisy, busy street)? Not a word of apology, no tone of contrition.

Now what was a mild annoyance—that it's 74F degrees when you like to sleep at 69F—is suddenly the end of the world! You swell with righteous fury, swear you'll write a letter to management, and savage the hotel in your online review.

Jean-Louis Gassée, who used to run Apple France, describes this situation as the choice between two tokens. When you deal with people who have trouble, you can either choose to take the token that says "It's no big deal" or the token that says "It's the end of the world." Whichever token you pick, they'll take the other.

The hotel staff in the example above clearly took the "It's no big deal" token and as a result forced you to take the "It's the end of the world" token. But they could just as well have made the opposite choice.

Imagine the staff answering something like this: "We're so sorry. That's clearly unacceptable! I can completely understand how it must be almost impossible to sleep when it's so hot in your room. If I can't fix this problem for you tonight, would you like me to re-fund your stay and help you find a different hotel room nearby? In any case, while we're figuring out the solution, allow me to send up a bottle of ice water and some ice cream. We're terribly sorry for this ordeal and we'll do everything to make it right."

With an answer like that, you're almost forced to pick the "It's no big deal" token. Yeah, sure, some water and ice cream would be great!

Everyone wants to be heard and respected. It usually doesn't cost much to do, either. And it doesn't really matter all that much whether you ultimately think you're right and they're wrong. Arguing with heated feelings will just increase the burn.

Keep that in mind the next time you take a token. Which one are you leaving for the customer?

The good old days

Just a few years ago we made a number of different products. Today we make just one: Basecamp. We gave up everything else—and the potential of millions more in revenue—so we could focus in rather than pan wide.

Companies typically downsize their offerings when they're not doing well. We did the opposite. We cut back in the best of times. At the moment we scaled back, business had never been better.

You don't hear about that a lot in business. Turning down growth, turning down revenue. Companies are culturally and structurally encouraged to get bigger and bigger.

But over the years we've talked to many entrepreneurs stuck in always-in-growth mode. And while many of them are proud of what they've achieved, just as many speak with longing in their voices about the good old days when their business was simpler and smaller. The days with less complexity, hassle, and headaches.

As we continued to hear fellow entrepreneurs reminiscing about the good old days, the more we kept thinking, "Why didn't they just grow slower and stay closer to the size they enjoyed the most?" Whatever the pressures, there's no law of nature dictating that businesses must grow quickly and endlessly. There's only a bunch of business-axiom baloney like "If you're not growing, you're dying." Says who?

We decided that if the good old days were so good, we'd do our best to simply settle there. Maintain a sustainable, manageable size. We'd still grow, but slowly and in control. We'd stay in the good days—no need to call them old anymore.

So we've decided to stay as small as we can for as long as we can. Rather than continue to invent new products, take on more responsibilities, and grow more obligations, we continually aim to pare down and lighten the load—even when times are great. Cutting back when times are great is the luxury of a calm, profitable, and independent company.

Today we're more like we were 12 years ago than we were 5 years ago. Intentionally. It feels great. All the while, we've been keeping healthy profits, increasing our benefits for our employees, and creating an environment where people can do the best work of their careers.

There's nothing old or crazy about that.

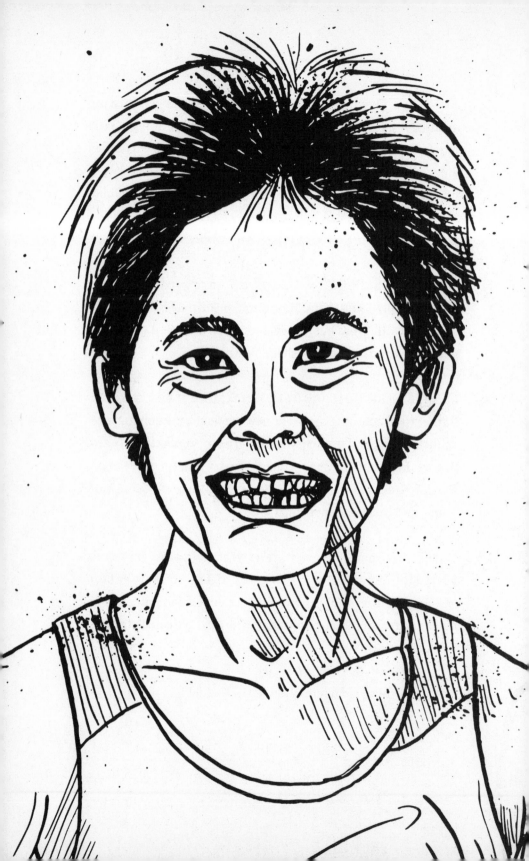

JAPANESE MARATHON RUNNER
YUKI KAWAUCHI, WHO WON THE
2018 BOSTON MARATHON, TRAINS
JUST ONCE A DAY BECAUSE HE
HAS A FULL-TIME GOVERNMENT
JOB AND BELIEVES IN
RESPECTING HIS BODY'S NATURAL
"MILEAGE LIMIT."

Last

Choose calm

A business is a collection of choices. Every day is a new chance to make a new choice, a different choice.

Are you going to continue to let people chip away at other people's time? Or are you going to choose to protect people's time and attention?

Are you going to keep trying to squeeze 10-hour days or 60-plus hours a week out of people? Or are you going to choose to make a reasonable number of hours count for more?

Are you going to continue to force people to pay attention to a dozen real-time conversations all day long? Or are you going to choose to relieve people from the conveyor belts of information and give them the focus that their best work requires?

Are you going to continue to expect people to respond immediately to everything? Or are you going to choose contemplation and consideration prior to communication?

Are you going to continue to burn more money than you earn, hoping that one day profit will finally materialize? Or are you going to choose to give endless growth a rest until the numbers work?

Are you going to continue to pile on more work and repeatedly miss deadlines? Or are you going to choose to give teams control over what can be reasonably accomplished given the time?

Are you going to keep pulling people off one incomplete thing to jump onto another incomplete thing? Or are you going to choose to finish what you started before moving on to the next?

Are you going to continue to say "That would never work in our business"? Are you going to continue to say "If the client calls at 11 p.m., I have to answer the phone"? Are you going to continue to say "It's okay to ask someone to work while they're on their vacation"? Or are you going to finally choose to make a change?

You have a choice. And if you don't have the power to make things change at the company level, find your local level. You always have the choice to change yourself and your expectations. Change the way you interact with people. Change the way you communicate. Start protecting your own time.

No matter where you live in an organization, you can start making better choices. Choices that chip away at crazy and get closer to calm.

A calm company is a choice. Make it yours.

Thanks for reading.

EVEN WITH EVERYTHING
OPRAH'S INVOLVED WITH,
SHE STILL TAKES TIME TO
MEDITATE, WALK HER DOGS,
AND SPEND TIME IN
HER GARDEN.

Bibliography

Isabel Allende

Salter, Jessica. "Inside Isabel Allende's World: Writing, Love and Rag Dolls." *The Telegraph*, April 19, 2013. https://www.telegraph.co.uk/culture/books/authorinterviews/10003099/Inside-Isabel-Allendes-world-writing-love-and-rag-dolls.html. Accessed June 2018.

Maya Angelou

Currey, Mason, ed. *Daily Rituals: How Artists Work*. New York: Alfred A. Knopf, 2013.

Yvon Chouinard

Welch, Liz. "The Way I Work: Yvon Chouinard, Patagonia." *Inc.*, March 12, 2013. https://www.inc.com/magazine/201303/liz-welch/the-way-i-work-yvon-chouinard-patagonia.html. Accessed June 2018.

Brunello Cucinelli

Malik, Om. "Brunello Cucinelli." *Pico*. https://pi.co/brunello-cucinelli-2/. Accessed June 2018.

Charles Darwin

Currey, Mason, ed. *Daily Rituals: How Artists Work*. New York: Alfred A. Knopf, 2013.

Dunne, Carey. "Charles Darwin and Charles Dickens Only Worked Four Hours a Day—and You Should Too." *Quartz*, March 22, 2017. https://qz.com/937592/rest-by-alex-soojung-kim-pang-the-daily-routines-of-historys-greatest-thinkers-make-the-case-for-a-four-hour-workday/. Accessed June 2018.

Simone de Beauvoir

Gobeil, Madeleine. "Simone de Beauvoir, The Art of Fiction No. 35." *The Paris Review*, Spring–Summer 1965. https://www.theparisreview.org/interviews/4444/simone-de-beauvoir-the-art-of-fiction-no-35-simone-de-beauvoir. Accessed June 2018.

Charles Dickens

Andrews, Evan. "8 Historical Figures with Unusual Work Habits." History.com, January 20, 2015. https://www.history.com/news/8-historical-figures-with-unusual-work-habits. Accessed June 2018.

Sandra Faber

Annual Reviews. *An Interview with Sandra Faber* (podcast). Annual Reviews Audio. Available at http://www.annualreviews.org/userimages/Content Editor/1299600853298/SandraFaberInterviewTranscript.pdf. Accessed June 2018.

Atul Gawande

Cunningham, Lillian. "Atul Gawande on the Ultimate End Game." *The Washington Post*, October 16, 2014. https://www.washingtonpost.com/news/on-leadership/wp/2014/10/16/atul-gawande-on-what-leadership-means-in-medicine/?utm_term=.8a7ee359539e. Accessed June 2018.

Stephen Hawking

Newport, Cal. "Stephen Hawking's Productive Laziness." *Study Hacks Blog*, January 11, 2017. http://calnewport.com/blog/2017/01/11/stephen-hawkings-productive-laziness/. Accessed June 2018.

Yuki Kawauchi

Barker, Sarah. "What the World's Most Famous Amateur Can Teach Pro Runners." *Deadspin*, January 9, 2018. https://deadspin.com/yuki-kawauchi-can-teach-you-how-to-run-1821725233. Accessed June 2018.

Tony Kushner

Brodsky, Katherine. "Fast Scenes, Slow Heart." *Stage Directions: The Art and Technology of Theatre*, March 31, 2010. http://stage-directions.com/current-issue/106-plays-a-playwriting/2258-fast-scenes-slow-heart.html. Accessed June 2018.

Gustav Mahler

Eichler, Jeremy. "Glimpsing Mahler's Music in Its Natural Habitat." *The Boston Globe*, April 7, 2016. https://www.bostonglobe.com/arts/music/2016/04/07/glimpsing-mahler-music-its-native-habitat/JlZewrlLp6fIiOgpUDwoLO/story.html#. Accessed June 2018.

van der Waal van Dijk, Bert. "1893–1896 Hotel Zum Hollengebirge (Composing cottage)." Gustav-Mahler.eu, February 12, 2017. https://www.gustav-mahler.eu/index.php/plaatsen/168-austria/steinbach-am-attersee/3255-composing-cottage. Accessed June 2018.

Haruki Murakami

Wray, John. "Haruki Murakami, The Art of Fiction No. 182." *The Paris Review*, Summer 2004. https://www.theparisreview.org/interviews/2/haruki-murakami-the-art-of-fiction-no-182-haruki-murakami. Accessed June 2018.

Shonda Rhimes

McCorvey, J. J. "Shonda Rhimes' Rule of Work: 'Come Into My Office with a Solution, Not a Problem.'" *Fast Company*, November 27, 2016. https://www.fastcompany.com/3065423/shonda-rhimes. Accessed June 2018.

Alice Waters

Hambleton, Laura. "Chef Alice Waters Assesses Benefits of Old Age." *The Washington Post*, November 18, 2013. https://www.washingtonpost.com/national/health-science/chef-alice-waters-assesses-benefits-of-old-age/2013/11/18/321e993a-1a37-11e3-82ef-a059e54c49d0_story.html. Accessed June 2018.

Colson Whitehead

Whitehead, Colson. "I'm Author Colson Whitehead—Just Another Down on His Luck Carny with a Pocketful of Broken Dreams—AMA." Reddit, March 26, 2018. https://www.reddit.com/r/books/comments/878ytl/im_author_colson_whitehead_just_another_down_on/. Accessed June 2018.

Oprah Winfrey

Silva-Jelly, Natasha. "A Day in the Life of Oprah." *Harper's Bazaar*, February 26, 2018. https://www.harpersbazaar.com/culture/features/a15895631/oprah-daily-routine/. Accessed June 2018.

Resources

Email us
So, what did you think of the book? Let us know at calm@basecamp.com. We read every email, and we'll do our best to respond.

Find us on Twitter
On Twitter we're at @jasonfried for Jason Fried, @dhh for David Heinemeier Hansson, and @basecamp for the company.

Check out Basecamp, the product
Used by over 100,000 companies worldwide, Basecamp is the calmer way to organize work, manage projects, and streamline communication companywide. Sign up for a free trial at basecamp.com.

Read our employee handbook
Our values, our structure, our methods, our benefits, and more are online for everyone to see at basecamp.com/handbook.

Browse our *Signal v. Noise* blog
We share new ideas and opinions regularly on our blog, *Signal v. Noise*. You can find that publication at signalvnoise.com.

Subscribe to our occasional email newsletter
About once a month we update everyone on what's new at Basecamp. Subscribe at http://basecamp.com/newsletter.

Other books we've written
Find a list of our other books at basecamp.com/books.

Watch some videos
Check out a wide variety of talks from Jason, David, and others on the Basecamp staff at basecamp.com/speaks.

Know your company
Knowyourcompany.com helps business owners get to know their employees better and overcome company growing pains.

More about us
Learn more at basecamp.com/about and basecamp.com/team.

Dedication

From Jason Fried:
To my family, to opportunity, and to luck—I'm fortunate to have you. Love and thanks.

From David Heinemeier Hansson:
To Jamie, Colt, and Dash for the love that gives patience and perspective to seek calm at work.

About the Authors

Jason Fried is the cofounder and CEO of Basecamp. He started the company back in 1999 and has been running the show ever since. Along with David, he wrote *Getting Real, REWORK,* and *REMOTE*. When it comes to business, he thinks things are simple until you make them complicated. And when it comes to life, we're all just trying to figure it out as we go.

David Heinemeier Hansson is the cofounder of Basecamp and the *New York Times* bestselling coauthor of *REWORK* and *REMOTE*. He's also the creator of the software toolkit Ruby on Rails, which has been used to launch and power Twitter, Shopify, GitHub, Airbnb, Square, and over a million other web applications. Originally from Denmark, he moved to Chicago in 2005 and now divides his time between the US and Spain with his wife and two sons. In his spare time, he enjoys 200-mph race cars in international competition, taking cliché pictures of sunsets and kids, and ranting far too much on Twitter.

HarperCollins books may be purchased for educational, business, or sales promotional use. For information, please email the Special Markets Department at SPsales@harpercollins.com.

FIRST EDITION

Grateful acknowledgment is made for permission to reprint from "What Light"
Words and Music by Jeff Tweedy, © 2007 Words Ampersand Music (BMI) / Poeyfarre Music (BMI) / Pear Blossom Music (BMI).
All Rights Administered by BMG Rights Management (US) LLC.
Used with Permission. All Rights Reserved.

Illustrations by Jason Zimdars

Library of Congress Cataloging-in-Publication Data
Names: Fried, Jason, author. | Hansson, David Heinemeier, author.
   Title: It doesn't have to be crazy at work / Jason Fried and David Heinemeier
   Hansson.
Description: First edition. | New York : HarperBusiness [2018] | Includes
   bibliographical references.
Identifiers: LCCN 2018028691 | ISBN 9780062874788 (hardcover)
Subjects: LCSH: Organizational behavior. | Organizational effectiveness. |
   Management.
Classification: LCC HD58.7 .F78 2018 | DDC 650.1—dc23 LC record available at
   https://lccn.loc.gov/2018028691

18 19 20 21 22   LSC   10 9 8 7 6 5 4 3 2 1